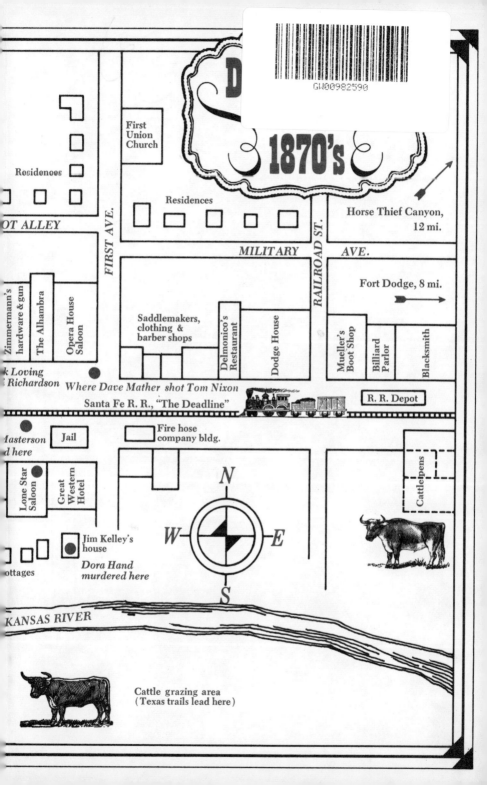

1870's

Residences

First Union Church

Residences

Horse Thief Canyon, 12 mi.

FIRST AVE.

RAILROAD ST.

MILITARY AVE.

OT ALLEY

Fort Dodge, 8 mi.

Zimmermann's hardware & gun

The Alhambra

Opera House Saloon

Saddlemakers, clothing & barber shops

Delmonico's Restaurant

Dodge House

Mueller's Boot Shop

Billiard Parlor

Blacksmith

k Loving Richardson

Where Dave Mather shot Tom Nixon

Santa Fe R. R., "The Deadline"

R. R. Depot

Masterson d here

Jail

Fire hose company bldg.

Lone Star Saloon

Great Western Hotel

Cattlepens

N

W — E

S

Jim Kelley's house

Dora Hand murdered here

ottages

KANSAS RIVER

Cattle grazing area
(Texas trails lead here)

Cowboy Capital of the World

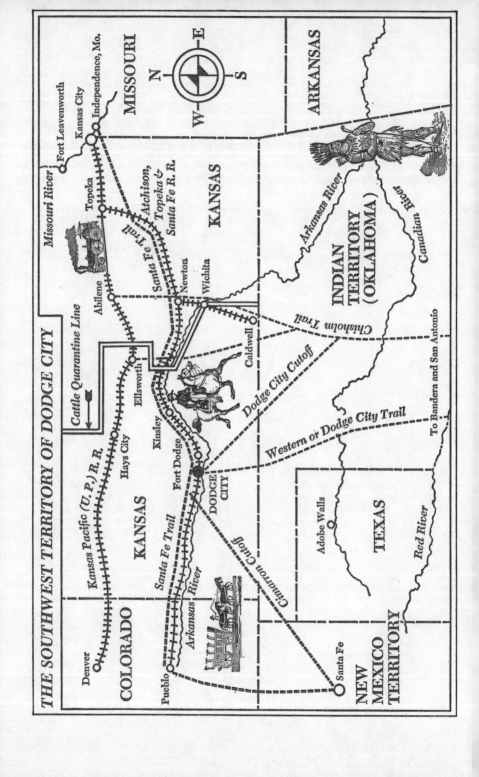

Cowboy Capital
of the World

THE SAGA OF DODGE CITY

By Samuel Carter III

DOUBLEDAY & COMPANY, INC.
GARDEN CITY, NEW YORK

ISBN: 0-385-05192-1 TRADE
0-385-05916-7 PREBOUND
LIBRARY OF CONGRESS CATALOG CARD NUMBER 72-90046

To Jane R. Robison, Betty Braddock, and Nina Jean Covalt *Gracious guardians of Dodge City's past*

"We had a frontier once. It was our most priceless possession. . . . It was there we showed our fighting edge, our unconquerable resolution, our undying faith. There, for a time, we were Americans."

EMERSON HOUGH

Contents

1

Crossroads of the Frontier

We cross the prairie as of old
The Pilgrims crossed the sea,
To make the West, as they the East,
The homestead of the Free!
Song of the Kansas Emigrant

"Out where the West begins" is, and was, a vague, romantic phrase, enduring today in history and legend.

But in the years immediately following the War Between the States it meant what long had been known as the Great American Desert—the level plateau stretching from the Missouri River to the Rockies, sparsely settled, inadequately charted and explored. Its keystone was the state of Kansas, admitted to the Union in 1861, across which the pioneer settlers moved westward with their wagon trains along ill-marked trails toward an irresistible but unknown destiny.

Geographically, the center of this frontier territory could be pinpointed at the Cimarron Crossing, where the westward trails forded the Arkansas River and continued on to Texas and New Mexico. Here, in due time, was the site of Dodge City, Queen of the Cowtowns, Cowboy Capital of the World, and (to some) the "wickedest city in the West."

Dodge, as the name was shortened by its citizens, could not lay sole claim to these titles. Before its Golden Decade of 1872–82 began, there were other raucous, prosperous cowtowns which preceded it—notably Abilene, Wichita, and Ellsworth. But for longer than its rivals, Dodge flourished as the typical, untamed frontier community, its founders typical of the men who conquered and settled and left their mark upon the Great Plains.

The term "Great Plains" was a far more appropriate name than Great American Desert for that Southwest part of Kansas which was then the crossroads of the vast expanding West. There were really two Kansases, two equal halves, different in topography and vegetation. An imaginary rule drawn perpendicularly through the state, the ninety-eighth meridian to be exact, was the approximate dividing line. East of that line were rolling woodlands, verdant fields, blue lakes and streams. Westward, the Great Plains began, treeless and sparsely irrigated, carpeted with short sweet grass that changed color with the seasons.

The state sloped slightly from west to east like a

tilted platform, twenty-five hundred feet above sea level at its center. Over it swept the winds of the jet stream, constant as the equatorial trades, rising sometimes to gale force, churning up dust and sand and heralding extremes of changing weather. From these penetrating winds the state got its name, Kansas being an Indian word meaning "People of the South Wind." The Arkansas River (pronounced Ar-*kan*-sas, with the final "s" enunciated) divided the state almost diagonally—a sluggish waterway beset by bars and quicksand, half a mile wide at most and rarely deeper than a man's waist. South of the river and west of the ninety-eighth meridian lay desert country, baked dry and lifeless by the sun, and extending to Texas, Colorado, and New Mexico.

Once the Central Plains were the exclusive domain of the buffalo and the Indian, who lived in a fruitful ecological balance. The Indians had since been pushed and herded, from as far east as Florida, into an area covering roughly the present state of Oklahoma south of Kansas. Not that they meekly accepted this confinement, or respected the tricky white man's treaties that had brought them there. Though this so-called Indian Territory was their lawful home—for a while at least, until further betrayal would deprive them of it—the Plains tribes especially still roamed the prairies around the site of Dodge and were, in a sense, one reason for the town's location.

The earliest white men to trespass on the Plains were the Spanish Conquistadores of the sixteenth century coming up from the Central American isthmus and the Gulf, notably Cabeza de Vaca and Francisco Vásquez de Coronado. They did not tarry long in the neighborhood of Kansas; only long enough to discover that there were no golden cities such as they had been informed of by sly Indian guides. They did, however, bequeath something to the land, by leaving behind a large number of the thousand horses and five thousand cattle brought with them on their ships from Europe.

The next Europeans to set foot on the Plains came after the Louisiana Purchase, especially following the War of 1812, when a newly united and awakened nation turned its eyes toward the West. Gold had yet to be discovered in California; but the little city of Santa Fe in present-day New Mexico was a golden mecca for the Yankee trader and the Dixieland adventurer who beat a mule path to this Spanish capital. When in 1821 a former army captain, William Becknell, guided a modest caravan of merchandise from the Missouri border to Santa Fe, and returned with gold and silver bullion representing twenty times his original investment, the Santa Fe Trail became a national artery between the East and West. Along it came hundreds of thousands of dollars' worth of gold and furs and specie in return for Southern and New England merchandise.

The Santa Fe Trail, as one historian has pointed out, was no mere line of ruts connecting two cities and two cultures. It was a perilous course across a boundless sea of grass whose rolling swells were swept by storms and gales and hurricanes. The Great Plains were thought of as an ocean, on which explorers navigated by the stars as had the early mariners of southern Europe. Men referred to the Conestoga wagons as prairie schooners, and spoke of reaching their destination as "fetching port."

The wagons themselves were modeled after a longboat's hull, with rising bow and stern, and were completely watertight. There were no bridges over Western streams and rivers, and the wagons often had to be poled across. One Yankee inventor known as Windwagon Thomas rigged his Conestoga as a catboat, and sped across the prairies like the clippers yet to come. On a second cruise, the vessel went into a wheel-locked spin from which it never recovered, pitching its crew to the buffalo sod. But Windwagon Thomas set sail again, this time alone, on his way to Santa Fe—and disappeared entirely, a mystery that ended with the epitaph "lost at sea."

This colorful, daring life of mercantile adventure ended with the Civil War, when "Bleeding Kansas" lived through a climate of factional strife and violence that would carry through to later years. A new era was dawning, no less turbulent, but one in which Kansas would become more than ever the

Crossroads of the Frontier—key to the birth of a great new empire in the Southwest. More than any other name in Western history, Dodge City would become a symbol of that era—reflecting like a clear, well-focused picture its extraordinary history.

Three factors gave birth to Dodge City and its ultimate proud position on the Plains. First was its projected location on the Santa Fe Trail, close to the likeliest crossing of the Arkansas River for wagon trains coming from Missouri and the East.

Second was its position in dead center of the buffalo range, athwart the route of the animals' migrations north and south. If the buffalo should be exterminated, at first an unlikely possibility, the short and verdant grass would then become grazing land for sheep and cattle, and even arable farm land for grangers coming from the East.

Third, but closely related to the second factor, was the coming of the Atchison, Topeka & Santa Fe Railroad which provided an important terminal and shipping point for buffalo robes and hides, and for the Longhorn cattle coming up the several trails from Texas.

Considering the first of these factors, the Santa Fe Trail had, of course, been passing through the site of Dodge for nearly a century and a half. Surveyed by the United States Government in 1825, it eventually carried as much as a million dollars' worth of goods and specie between its Missouri terminal and Santa

Fe. To the marauding Comanches and Cheyennes, still lords of the Plains whatever others thought of them, the wagon trains were like the Spanish galleons to the pirates of the Caribbean. Time and again they raided the caravans, making off with the loot as it returned from Mexico, killing and scalping the drivers for good measure. A favorite point of ambush was the Cimarron Crossing, fifteen miles west of the site of Dodge, where the Conestoga wagons trying to ford the shallow Arkansas made an easy target for the raiders.

During the Civil War, when Union troops were engaged elsewhere, the raids increased in intensity. And immediately after the war, demand went up for greater protection for the merchant caravans and wagon trains that carried settlers westward in the great postwar migrations. Troops dispatched from distant forts like Leavenworth in northeast Kansas could make swift punitive attacks upon the Indians, but as soon as the soldiers returned to their posts the Indians were back again.

In 1867 General William T. Sherman, famed for his march through Georgia to the sea and then commander of the Southwest Military District, promoted the erection of Fort Dodge eight miles east of the site of Dodge City. The outpost was named for General Grenville M. Dodge, whose nephew, Major (later Colonel) Richard Irving Dodge, was the first commander of the fort. Initially it was little more than a collection of sod huts and enclosures perched close to the riverbank and ignoring, for the sake of a water supply, the safer, higher land in the interior. The fortification made this section of the Santa Fe considerably safer from attack by Indians and outlaws.

Sometimes, as the caravans passed westward toward the crossing, they were held up by herds of buffalo numbering in the tens of thousands. The shaggy beasts were a handy source of meat for the pioneers, as they had been a source of food to the Indians for centuries.

Later the herds provided meat for the army units patrolling the area, the work crews of the railroads in their race toward the Colorado border, and finally for the hunters who flocked toward the Great Plains for the greatest massacre of wildlife in the nation's history. When a Pennsylvania tanner perfected a means of processing buffalo hides into high-quality leather, the Great Buffalo Hunt reached massive proportions, bringing gunners, both professional and amateur, to the site of Dodge, in overwhelming numbers.

Meanwhile southern Texas was engaged in dealing with a different sort of cattle, the Spanish Longhorns. Bred in the wild from strains the Conquistadores had brought to the country and abandoned centuries before, the herds had reached seemingly inexhaustible proportions. Before the War Between the States they had been driven to markets in Missouri and Louisiana, returning a substantial profit to the drovers—an operation that was interrupted with the firing on Fort Sumter in the spring of 1861.

Now, the war over, with money short in Texas and the Longhorns roving free, the cattle could be corralled by any enterprising Texan. Steers that cost nothing, driven north and fattening on the open range, could bring fifteen dollars a head in Kansas City and St. Louis, thirty or forty dollars in the slaughterhouses of Chicago and New York. The only obstacles to their transportation to the shipping points were the hostile Indian territories where the tribes demanded a cut of the herds that passed across their land. Also, the difficult, ill-marked trails through the wilderness of Louisiana and Missouri took a heavy toll of animals and men.

It was an egotistical, imaginative man named Joseph G. McCoy who switched the Texas cattle drives to Kansas and made cowtown history. McCoy, only twenty-nine and slender with a pointed goatee to hide his age, was one of three brothers engaged in the livestock business in Springfield, Illinois. He saw the inexhaustible demand for meat in the populous East, if only a more convenient shipping point could be established closer to the Texas border. He went to Kansas to locate "a market whereat the southern drover and northern buyer would meet upon an equal footing and both be undisturbed by mobs or swindling thieves."

First making sure of rail connections from the Missouri River to Chicago, he persuaded officials of the Kansas Pacific ("Katy") Railroad, then pushing westward across the Plains, to establish a cattle shipping terminal at Abilene, complete with acres of stockyards, shipping pens, and hostelries for drovers. He selected Abilene, which he described as "a small, dead place, consisting of a dozen huts" because it was the nearest point beyond a line forbidding the import of Texas Longhorn steers into eastern Kansas—the Longhorns being suspected carriers of "Spanish fever" that was fatal to domestic Shorthorn cattle.

McCoy then sent an agent from Kansas to intercept the drovers bringing their herds north from Texas, and directed them to this new and promising facility. According to his own account, the cattlemen found the news "almost too good to believe; that someone was about to afford a Texas drover any other reception than outrage and robbery." Not overlooking the value of advertising, McCoy also organized the first touring Wild West Show, "a collection of three buffalo, an elk, and three wild ponies, all chased around an enclosure by a pair of costumed Mexican vaqueros before delighted audiences in St. Louis and Chicago."

Overnight Abilene became a center and a symbol

of the great new era for the Southwest. According to Professor Walter Prescott Webb in his peerless study *The Great Plains*, Abilene stood for all that happened when two great cultures met in conflict, the civilized East and the untamed, lawless West. "On the surface Abilene was corruption personified. Life was hectic, raw, lurid, awful. But the dance hall, the saloon, the red light, and the dissonance of immoral revelry punctuated by pistol shots, were but the superficialities of deeper forces working themselves out around the new town." These forces were the cowtowns' services in expanding the American frontier and opening the Great Southwest.

One could dwell long on the story of Abilene even though its boom-and-bust existence lasted only four short years. But much of that story was to be retold in Dodge, where many of Abilene's temporary citizens later arrived to replay their roles of lawmen, gunmen, gamblers, dance hall and saloon proprietors. Meanwhile the Kansas Pacific pushed on to Hays and Ellsworth, giving each a similar moment of glory before the silver rails moved farther west, to leave them dying on the vine. Contributing to their decline, and also under Joe McCoy's persuasion, a second railway had begun to parallel the Katy's route, farther south and closer to Texas: the Atchison, Topeka & Santa Fe.

Just as McCoy was considered the father of the Kansas cattle industry, the Santa Fe was the empire builder of the West. In time it would become the greatest railway network in the nation, feeding and milking the entire Southwest territory. Awarded extensive land grants by the government, on its promise to reach the Colorado border by the end of 1872, the Santa Fe survived not only by selling this land to settlers and supplying them with passage and provisions, but also by offering new points of shipment for the Longhorn cattle coming north from Texas.

The rivalry between these two main systems racing across Kansas to the Colorado border, as well as the fierce competition between wildcat railroads sprouting from them, led at times to bloody warfare. Work crews went armed, for protection against Indians and outlaws and to intercept and disrupt the work of rival crews. It was a type of destructive guerrilla war that each could little afford when faced with such common hazards as marauding Indians, treacherous riverbeds, drought and hunger and devastating storms. But the tracks went through; they had to go through, to fulfill their land-grant contracts.

Along the Santa Fe, as it moved south from Topeka to the Arkansas and then due west to Colorado, there sprang up a second chain of cowtowns similar to its sisters to the north—with a strip of barely a hundred miles between them. These later cattle centers were to have a marked advantage. In 1872 the

quarantine line against Texas cattle was moved farther west, placing the kiss of death on dying cities
such as Abilene. In proportionate degree the move
brought sudden fame to wild and woolly Wichita,
which became a prototype of the cowtowns of the
future, these in turn becoming models for Dodge
City.

Ruled by one of the earliest of Western marshals,
Wild Bill Hickok, Wichita was briefly everything
that Dodge was destined to become: a wide-open
town that took the law into its own hands, primed
with free-flowing money from the cattle trade, and
inundated by hordes of gamblers, gunmen, outlaws,
rustlers, and ladies of easy virtue, not to mention the
Texas cowboys who drove their herds to the camps
outside the city and then took over the town with
pockets full of four to six months' wages itching to
be spent on liquor, women, dice, and whatever
high-spirited entertainment they could unearth or
invent.

In Wichita as in Abilene, but in greater numbers,
appeared many of the dramatic personalities that
would later play their parts in Dodge: sheriffs and
marshals like Bat Masterson, Jack Bridges, Billy
Tilghman, Charlie Bassett, and Wyatt Earp; hunters
like Buffalo Bill Cody, Billy Dixon, and Kirk Jordan;
cattle barons like Abel "Shanghai" Pierce; gunmen
like the Thompson brothers, Billy and Ben, Wesley
Hardin, and Clay Allison; professional gamblers like

Luke Short, Doc Holliday, and Phil Coe. Whichever side they were on, whether that of law and order or lawlessness, they helped make Dodge City the undisputed capital of the Southwest in the years to come.

Again the railroad tracks moved west and Wichita's boom years began to fade. Detouring briefly to Caldwell, the Santa Fe moved to and through its later offspring, Newton, Hutchinson, and Kinsley—and finally to the newly christened Dodge in August 1872. Here it was welcomed "with a shout that could be heard around the world," recorded Robert M. Wright, one of the founders of the town. "This will be the greatest city the West has ever known," asserted its local boomers. With some qualifications, they were right.

The story of Dodge is not the story of a single city. It is a capsule history of the West—of the pioneer towns that shaped and sustained the great frontier from the Mississippi and Missouri to the Rockies. While it had much in common with such mining camps as Deadwood, Tombstone, and Virginia City, the raw materials with which it worked were different, far more basic to America—the range, the buffalo herds, the horse, the rifle, and the Longhorn cattle. It was as big in heart and spirit as the space around it. "There is room for only one Dodge in Kansas," wrote a Western editor. He was right. It was hard enough, as history proved, to keep that single little city from exploding at the seams.

If the story of Dodge is, in many chapters, one of lawlessness and violence, of loose irreverence and immorality, of vice and greed, one must judge these things in context, see the picture as a whole. For there was also loyalty, self-sacrifice, and generosity; extraordinary bravery at times, and even faith. The people of Dodge faced up to incredible hardships, dangers, fears, and deprivations—relying on courage and resourcefulness in an environment which offered little else to count on. They not only survived—they survived with a smile, a shrug, and an enduring sense of humor.

Perhaps the legacy that Dodge has left to the nation—one legacy, at any rate—is summed up in the motto of the state of Kansas, *Ad astra per aspera:* Through difficulty to the stars.

2

Buffalo City

Oh, the days of elk and buffalo!
It fills my heart with pain
To know those days are past and gone
To never come again.
Old Scout's Lament

There were years, old-timers of Dodge recalled, when the brown-green prairies on both sides of the Arkansas trembled beneath the hoofbeats of millions of buffalo. North and south from Canada to southern Texas the buffalo range stretched for fifteen hundred miles, five hundred miles in width from the Missouri to the Rockies.

Largest of animals indigenous to North America, the buffalo had been there for more centuries than anybody knew. They were observed of course by the treasure-hunting Coronado, who spoke of "stopping to hunt cows on the way," and had been sighted earlier by Cabeza de Vaca—a name appropriately meaning "Head of the Cow"—who described them as "native cows, some tawny and some black." But it was the early French *voyageurs* who gave them their American name (properly they are bison), calling them *les boeufs,* or beeves, which the Anglo-Saxons twisted to *buffle* and then buffalo.

How many were there? No one really knew for sure. They blanketed the prairies like a living robe, black and shaggy and forever on the move in quest of grass and water. The most reliable estimates placed the overall herd at between sixty and seventy million, reduced to some forty million by the time that Dodge was born. Robert M. Wright, an early settler at Fort Dodge, reported riding through a herd two hundred miles in length, "as close together as herded cattle." With appropriate awe he added, "The whole face of the earth was covered with buffalo."

Anyone in the vicinity of Fort Dodge in 1869 and 1870 might have come to the same conclusion. The Plains on both sides of the Arkansas teemed and thundered with buffalo, pocked with the sun-reflecting buffalo wallows where they rolled and pawed the dust. The plunging of herds that forded the river sounded like a waterfall. The bulls weighed as much as sixteen hundred pounds—sometimes more than a ton—and stood from five to six feet high measured from their humps. Seemingly indestructible, they were truly the Monarchs of the Plains.

To the Plains Indians, especially the Cheyennes and the Comanches, the buffalo had been for centuries a source of life, and hunting them a lifetime occupation. The buffalo provided not only food, since the nomadic tribes planted no crops, but many other articles essential to existence. The shaggy skins were used for clothes and blankets, the tanned hides for shelters and tepees and moccasins. The tendons provided strings for their bows, the horns and bones were fashioned into tools. Even the buffalo chips provided fuel for cooking and for warmth in winter. A robe from the rare albino buffalo was worn by Indian chiefs in battle as a charm against enemy missiles, while medicine men used the white robes to effect miraculous cures.

The mounted tribes, on mustangs whose clipped ears marked them as "buffalo ponies," pursued the herds on horseback, shooting on the run. Others stalked them on foot, driving them into cul-de-sacs, or stampeding the animals over cliffs. But this was not the useless slaughter which the white man practiced. To the Indian, the buffalo was too precious to kill for sport. The civilization of the Plains Indians was based on the buffalo, just as that of the Eastern tribes was based on maize, or corn.

Then came the white man with gunpowder, shells, and rifles. True, the early pioneers and settlers regarded the buffalo primarily as a source of food. Many future citizens of Dodge supplied the wagon trains and the railroad crews, as well as the later town itself, with meat. Some hunted with old army rifles, many of them muzzle-loaders, until the Sharps fifty came into common use. It could hurl a heavy slug seven hundred yards, but had certain disadvantages. It was expensive; the octagonal barrel quickly became overheated; it was not too accurate. And it was heavy.

As game, the buffalo was considered a somewhat stupid animal, with poor sight, slow reflexes, and a clumsy and ungainly gait. But its ponderous movement was deceptive; it could often outrun an uninitiated pony. Its sense of smell was keen, and a herd could only be approached downwind. Moreover, the buffalo was hard to kill. Its tough hide could absorb innumerable bullets. Only a clean shot through the head or neck was mortal. A wounded bull might turn with fury on its pursuer, dispose of the horse with a quick thrust of its mighty neck and horns, then gore or trample the rider to death. Many a greenhorn met with such a fate.

As a convenient center of the range, on the path of the great migrations north and south, the site of Dodge became a mecca for buffalo hunters from the frontier cities to the east. Many had already established enviable records. William ("Buffalo Bill") Cody, shooting from the saddle, bagged sixty-nine buffalo in a single morning in the sight of a mounted audience which treated him to a champagne lunch.

While still in his early twenties Wyatt Earp, a disciple of Cody's who had moved west with his family from Illinois, settled for a daily score of eighteen to twenty-eight head, also shooting from the saddle.

Many were drawn to the area by the sheer thrill of the chase. For years old-timers talked of the royal hunt held for the Grand Duke Alexis of Russia, led by Dodge's scout and marksman, Brick Bond. But increasingly the goal became dollars-and-cents profit. Buffalo meat had long been the staple of pioneer settlers, wagon trains, and railroad working crews. It was succulent, tender if properly butchered, and not unsimilar in taste to beef. Shortly, demand for buffalo meat spread east to Kansas City and St. Louis, even to restaurants in Chicago and New York.

Fives miles west of Fort Dodge on the banks of the Arkansas the first sod house was built by Henry L. Stitler, a government teamster, providing a sort of dormitory and supply base for the hunters. Charley Meyers, a veteran buffalo hunter, established a trading post adjoining. Around these sprang up canvas tents and wickiups and assorted shelters built of hides. An enterprising pioneer named George M. Hoover erected a frame-and-hide saloon and wholesale liquor store, around which burgeoned other tent saloons and gambling shacks. These marks of civilization, plus the knowledge that the Atchison, Topeka & Santa Fe was pushing toward the camp, seemed to demand a name for the community. It was christened, logically, Buffalo City.

It was an unpretentious little settlement. With no wood available for lumber, and few willing to take the time to build enduring huts of sod, most of the dwellings were thrown together with poles and buffalo skins. The hides, it was found, if laid flat in the sun to dry, would harden like planks, and could be used for floors and roofing and even bar tops for the burgeoning saloons.

Around this makeshift city on the prairies, the Great Buffalo Hunt of the 1870s reached its zenith. The Monarchs of the Plains became the raw material of a gigantic business. On top of the demand for meat in Eastern markets rose a sudden clamor for buffalo robes. The shaggy pelts became faddishly popular for coats, for hats, for carpeting, for blankets. Hardly a fashionable parlor in the East was without its buffalo skins to spread before the hearth. Few passengers traveled abroad by carriage or sleigh without a buffalo robe to spread across the knees.

Sports-minded hunters like Charlie Rath, one of the early settlers of the town, Wyatt Earp, and Buffalo Bill Cody, pursued the buffalo on horseback. But the professionals, intent on mass production, took no such sporting chances. The buffalo might charge a mounted man but tended to ignore a man on foot. The average hunter shot from a "stand," a position downwind from the herd, bracing his

Sharps fifty rifle on a forked stick. He was accompanied by three or four skinners (the professional hunter disdained the messy task of skinning the carcasses) and at least two wagons by which to haul the day's kill back to camp.

It was, in general, a safe and easy operation. A marksman skilled in buffalo lore knew how to single out his prey without causing the whole herd to stampede—the major danger. The buffaloes were curiously indifferent to a fallen comrade as well as to the sound of the gunshot. If the obvious leader of the herd was brought down first, the others would tend to crowd around him in bewilderment, to be picked off one by one. If they moved away at all it was only slowly; the marksman rarely had to change position.

Theoretically there was no limit to the buffalo that could be slaughtered by this method. But practically, around fifty was the maximum number which the skinners could attend to in a single day (twice that amount with a pair of hunters and double the number of skinners). The hunter would reach his quota by midmorning, then stand watch for Indians who might have been alerted by the shooting, while the skinners finished up their work. Then hides and carcasses were loaded on the wagons and the party returned to Wright's or Rath's depots on the outskirts of the city.

Even at this stage, with hides selling at one to

three dollars each, a hunter could make from fifty to a hundred dollars a day, with skinners receiving slightly less. Buffalo City attracted hordes of fortune-seeking hunters, as had the California Gold Rush days of 1849. Many were characters destined to play significant roles in the future drama of Dodge City. Among them was young Bill Tilghman, one of the crack shots of the range, a tall lanky lad of eighteen with flowing black locks, who had been supplying meat to the advancing railroad crews. Now he and his partner George Rust stepped up production, delivering three or four thousand pounds of meat a day to Buffalo City. Red-headed Brick Bond reported killing three hundred buffalo in a single day, but his record was challenged by Tom Nixon, who claimed shooting 120 buffalo from a single stand in forty minutes, bagging 2173 in less than five weeks.

Although Charlie Rath continued to hunt buffalo on the Plains, he teamed with Bob Wright to form the firm of Rath & Wright, the first permanent mercantile establishment in the city, dealing in buffalo meat and hides. Most of the hunters worked for, and were supplied by, Rath & Wright. John Mooar, a former woodcutter from Vermont, who delivered skins to the store at $2.25 per hide, described the typical hunter's procedure:

> At nine o'clock by the watch I left camp. I didn't calculate to shoot the gun off before ten o'clock ne'er

a time. I went out on horseback ahead of my three wagons and my skinners followed me. I calculated to find some buffalo sometime between nine and ten o'clock when it was getting warm. I wasn't in no hurry in the morning and I generally did all my shooting by noon. Then I'd sit up on a high hill somewhere while my men were scattering around doing the skinning. I kept watch to see that nobody bothered them.

It was not always that simple or that safe. Hunters were killed or trampled by stampeding buffalo. The Plains Indians, theoretically confined to Indian Territory, hunted freely on the prairies and made frequent hit-and-run attacks on those who threatened them with competition. Then there were the bitter blizzards to contend with. With no refrigeration, winter was the time for killing buffalo, since the meat remained frozen while awaiting shipment.

During the settlement's first big season Major Richard Dodge reported that "more than a hundred buffalo hunters were frozen to death along the Arkansas. The post surgeon at the fort performed seventy amputations on frost bitten hunters. More than two hundred lost hands or feet or other extremities." But the hunters were a hardy lot. One who lost both hands and feet, according to the major, was back in a few months "attending to his duties," though the officer did not mention what those duties were.

Still the slaughter not only continued but accelerated, due to two major developments. Hitherto, tanning had been a local craft, involving simply proper soaking, scraping, and drying (Indian women often chewed the hides to make them soft). But in Philadelphia in 1871 two German tanners developed a method of processing buffalo hides into leather for use in boots and shoes and, even more important, belting for machines and factories. The price of hides in Buffalo City jumped to three, four, and five dollars per skin or even higher.

During that summer, too, the Santa Fe Railroad approached the site in a race to meet its deadline for transversing Kansas. Merchants like Rath and Wright, George Hoover, and other early settlers started investing heavily in real estate, seeing a golden future for the city. The Postmaster General in Washington took notice of the burgeoning community and objected to its adopted name. Kansas already had two settlements, named Buffalo and Buffalo Station. It was too confusing. The citizens agreed and, out of consideration for the fort, renamed their little metropolis Dodge City.

The Santa Fe's chief engineer, Albert A. Robinson, surveyed and plotted the town in tidy squares, with its principal thoroughfare, Front Street, paralleling the projected railroad tracks. To plan and finance the operation a Town Company was formed consisting of leading settlers and officers of the Fort, and headed by Colonel Richard Irving Dodge. Construction gangs working for the railroad filled the vacant spaces with their tents and shacks, expanding the "canvas and tarpaper town."

Among these work crews was a tow-haired, blue-eyed youngster named Bill Masterson and his older brother Ed. Both had fled the boredom of their family's farm in eastern Kansas to seek adventure in this rising frontier town. Bill (later "Bat") Masterson lost no time in making a reputation for himself. When Boss Ritter, the contractor, tried to leave town without paying the Mastersons their wages, Bill borrowed enough money from Tom Nixon for a Colt six-shooter, ambushed Ritter in a railroad car, and collected their three hundred dollars pay at gunpoint. The Masterson name gained instant recognition in Dodge City.

On September 19 the first train of banana-yellow cars and tulip-funneled locomotive snorted into Dodge over the wobbly, slightly raised tracks of the Santa Fe. "It wasn't much of a train," recorded one grizzly hunter among the throng of welcomers, "but it sure caused a big celebration." Significantly, it had been delayed two hours while a herd of buffalo ten miles long and three miles wide plodded across the track. The column appeared to "number in the millions." According to one report, "Men from the train took pot shots at the nearest buffaloes. So many of the wounded were trampled to death that, after the herd had cleared the track, about five hundred carcasses were left on the prairie."

The senseless slaughter was an omen of the future. A passenger in the cars, who had crossed the Plains from Wichita to Dodge, reported that "from the way the carcasses are strewn over the prairies, the American bison will soon be a thing of the past." How right he was!

There had been efforts by those ahead of their time to check the massacre. As early as 1872 the state legislature, and later the United States Congress, proposed measures to "prevent the wanton destruction of the buffalo." Both bills were vetoed. Colonel Richard Dodge, whose fort provided a grandstand view of the bloody circus, believed that "no legislation, however stringent, could do anything for or against the trade of buffalo products."

Though the name had been changed, Dodge was still *de facto* Buffalo City—the buffalo capital of the world. It was infected, all but delirious, with buffalo fever. The Santa Fe in its first three months after reaching Dodge, with only an empty boxcar for a depot, shipped more than forty-three thousand hides and one and a half million pounds of meat from the city. Mountains of buffalo steaks and tongues rose like frozen Matterhorns along the track, awaiting shipment to Chicago and New York. Stacks of hides, often worth a hundred thousand dollars, lined the railroad right-of-way.

Rath & Wright's store was the center of this booming trade. Bob Wright, now hailed as the "Merchant Prince of Dodge," observed:

> Hardly had the railroad reached the city, than business began. And what a business! Dozens of cars a day were loaded with hides and meat; while dozens of carloads of grain, flour, and provisions kept arriving every day. The streets of Dodge were lined with wagons, bringing in hides and meat and getting supplies from early morning to late at night. . . . I have been to several mining camps where rich strikes were made, but I never saw any town to equal Dodge.

Checking the records, Wright observed: "Charles Rath and I shipped over two hundred thousand buffalo hides the first winter the Atchison, Topeka, and Santa Fe Railroad reached Dodge City, and I think there were at least as many more shipped from there, besides two hundred cars of hind quarters and two cars of buffalo tongues." The yard erected beside Rath & Wright's rarely held less than seventy or eighty thousand hides stacked flat in giant ricks, and one surviving photograph shows partner Wright beside a mountain of forty thousand skins.

The big sensation of that first winter was the white buffalo robe brought in by Prairie Dog Dave Morrow —maverick scion of a prominent eastern family—first of its kind to be garnered by a white man, for which Rath & Wright paid a thousand dollars. Wright

shipped it to Kansas City, where for years it hung
on exhibition, attracting the curious and envious for
miles around. It ended up on permanent display in
the State Capitol at Topeka. What happened to all
the other buffalo robes, once numbering in the millions, that graced New England homes and com-
forted American travelers for generations remains a
mystery. Seemingly as indestructible as the buffalo
itself, only a token few remain.

Not all were as lucky as Prairie Dog Dave, but it
was a poor hunter who could not make from three
to five hundred dollars a day. During the season of
1873, half a million hides were shipped from Dodge,
along with eight hundred tons of meat. Buffalo
money poured into the city like an invigorating tonic.
With it came the gamblers and the shysters, shady
promoters, hunters, fortune seekers, prostitutes, and
gunmen. Many had not yet acquired notoriety, like
"Mysterious Dave" Mather (not to be confused with
Prairie Dog Dave), Dutch Henry, horse thief and
cattle rustler, and gunman Hank Brown, one of the
more ruthless killers of the West.

With lumber freighted to the city by the Santa Fe,
crude frame buildings were erected along Front
Street, with wooden sidewalks lining both sides of
the unpaved thoroughfare. Beebe's Iowa House on
Front Street claimed to be the city's first hotel.
Rath & Wright's was, for a while, the principal supply
store. Jerry-built dance halls, gambling parlors, and

saloons selling whiskey at thirty cents a drink sprang up like weeds, with hitching rails provided for their customers. Clogged with the wagons of freighters bearing bones and hides, it was dirty, smelly, noisy, and above all dusty—with the windblown dust covering buildings, horses, and people with a yellow pall.

The sound of gunplay soon became the theme song of Dodge City. Every day the Santa Fe brought still more hordes of hunters, to supplement the more or less permanent population of a thousand souls. Those who flocked to the platform to greet the westbound trains found exhilarating sport in trying to shoot out the headlights on the approaching locomotive—until the engineer learned to douse his lights on approaching Dodge and let the train coast well beyond the depot before unloading passengers and cargo.

The financial panic of 1873, which brought hardships to the eastern section of the nation, only further spurred the hunt for buffalo and the trade in meat and hides. As the herds became sorely depleted, and a plague of grasshoppers ravaged the grazing lands, a new source of income, a salvation to Dodge City, suddenly appeared.

All over the Plains millions of buffalo skeletons and bones lay bleaching in the sun. Hide-hunting might be on the decline, but here was the basis of a million-dollar business. Ex-hunters, homesteaders, and newly arrived settlers began gathering up the bones and hauling them by wagons to the railroad yard, to be shipped east for grinding into fertilizer or manufacturing bone china.

It took the skeletons of a hundred buffalo to make a ton of bones, worth eight dollars a load on delivery to the railroad agent—if the collectors were willing to make the arduous haul across the prairies. Enterprising traders like Charlie Rath sent wagons across the Plains offering on-the-spot payment of two dollars a ton for bones. Before delivery to the freight yard where the bones were weighed, each load was drenched with water. This increased the weight and raised the price to up to fourteen dollars.

As early as 1873 the Santa Fe shipped almost three million pounds of bones to Eastern markets. Buffalo bones, it was said irreverently, were as good as currency in Dodge, and the town that had once been celebrated as Buffalo City might well have assumed the title of Bone City. Just as stacks of hides had formerly lined the railroad tracks, now a mountain of bones, half a mile in length and ten feet high, rose along the right-of-way—a grim reminder that the buffalo had all but gone.

The passing of the buffalo was little mourned in Dodge or anywhere throughout the Southwest. For already the Longhorns were arriving, promising the same prosperity to Dodge that they had brought to Abilene and Wichita. There was not sufficient forage for both beeves and buffalo; the range had to be cleared for a more profitable breed of cattle. Wrote historian James Marshall:

> Romantically, perhaps it was too bad the buffalo had to go. But historically and economically it was inevitable. The prairies never could have been settled as long as seventy-five million huge grass eaters moved freely over them. Cattle drives would have been stalled and stampeded. The Santa Fe itself could not have been operated successfully if trains were forced to stop or inch their way through herds which no fence ever built could stop.

The commander at Fort Dodge, along with Southern generals Sheridan and Sherman, rationalized the slaughter of the buffalo with different reasoning. It helped to keep away the Indians, if not eliminate them altogether. Colonel Dodge insisted that "the Plains tribes could only be subdued if the herds were completely destroyed, thereby forcing the Indians to rely entirely on the government for provisions. The red men would undoubtedly not leave their reservations if the empty Plains, devoid of the last herd of bison, promised nothing more than slow starvation."

The buffalo era would not end for good until 1878, when Rath & Wright's last shipment totaled forty thousand hides. After that, as a sentimental token of the period, two tame buffalo were allowed to roam the streets of Dodge, fed and pampered like the sacred cows of India. While they sometimes

made a nuisance of themselves, frightening house-
wives, annoying strangers, charging the red flannel
underwear that hung from clotheslines, they were
cherished reminders of that day of primitive but
easy living. For the Longhorn cattle were arriving
now, and the city was facing up to new responsibil-
ities.

3

Growing Pains

Twenty saloons and a tin peeyanner,
  A gal or two in a calico gown,
Plenty of red-eye and some three-card monte,
  Put 'em all together and you've got a town.
  Cowboys Catchall of Song and Verse

He was a disconsolate cowboy down on his luck and
somewhat the worse for whiskey, riding the cars of
the Santa Fe to nowhere in particular. John Bender,
the conductor, tapped his shoulder.

"Where to?" asked Bender kindly.

"Goin' to hell, most likely," muttered the cowboy.

"That'll be two dollars, and get off at Dodge,"
John told him.

The story, often repeated till it joined the ranks
of legend, carried at least a grain of truth. For once
it got started, Dodge City lost no time in acquiring
its reputation as "the wickedest little city in the
West." Perhaps the boast was an exaggeration, touted

by citizens anxious to attract free-spending visitors. But the epithet of Helldorado that applied to early mining towns was equally applicable to Dodge.

The colonel at the fort was fond of recalling a perhaps more authentic story concerning the wagonload of Missouri emigrants traveling west on the Santa Fe Trail. Approaching Dodge, they applied to the fort's commander for an escort to accompany them through the modern Sodom and Gomorrah. The colonel sympathetically complied. Early next morning, after kneeling in prayer on the highway to beseech the Almighty to protect them from the fiends of Dodge, the caravan trundled warily down Front Street, then raced to the safety of the Plains.

As he later confessed, the colonel could have reassured the travelers that in the early-morning hours Dodge was as safe as a convent, for no gunman or gambler thought of getting up before midafternoon. But even the soldiers at Fort Dodge had reason to regard the surprising offspring at their knee as something of a problem child. In fact, before the town was officially established Colonel Richard Dodge, aware that it might include "rum shops and houses of ill repute," insisted that the city limits be kept at a safe distance from the fort.

One might cite the years 1873 to 1876 as marking the period of Dodge's adolescent but surprising growth. The original hub of six saloons, a couple of dance halls, and Rath & Wright's Supply House, grew like Topsy, and the population reached a thousand. In the next two years that figure doubled. Charlie Rath went out on his own to form Rath & Company, while Bob Wright teamed with Texas cattleman Henry Beverley to create Wright, Beverley & Company, one of the leading supply houses of the West.

Wright, Beverley & Company, besides offering everything from pins to portable houses, Studebaker wagons to "a festive Bowie Knife," also handled the town's financial transactions, for it would be another ten years before George Hoover helped to found the first Dodge City Bank. Close by stood Fred Zimmermann's hardware shop with its outsize rifle above the door announcing the sale of guns and ammunition, and John Mueller's "Sign of the Big Boot" whose merchandise needed no further advertisement. Down the street was Delmonico's "Restaurant for the Elite," while across the way ex-freighter Hamilton Bell built and ran the Elephant, largest livery stable in the state of Kansas.

Ham Bell—who also operated Dodge's funeral parlor, a busy institution in that trigger-happy town— deserved more than passing mention. He was one of the city's more lovable and generous personalities. The upstairs hayloft of the Elephant was open to all homeless travelers, and as many as fifty cowboys often bedded down there for the night. When a prophet with no respect for superstition warned that one of the cowboys, lighting a cigarette, might set the place ablaze, it promptly caught fire before the day was over.

Among his many philanthropic traits Bell was fond of distributing free buttermilk throughout the town to promote both the health and the virtue of its people. In a city dedicated to strong spirits, Ham optimistically patrolled the streets of Dodge with his bucket of buttermilk like Diogenes carrying his lamp through Athens in search of an honest man.

Front Street was actually a hundred-yard-wide plaza, and was so called, with the railroad tracks running down dead center. Along the false-front stores and business establishments on either side ran sidewalks of planks about eight feet wide, sheltered by wooden awnings. Emptied whiskey barrels filled with water were spaced along the sidewalk railings as the city's only firefighting measure. Later they were hoisted to the rooftops as a sort of self-releasing sprinkling system. If the roofs caved in from the flames the barrels would presumably be tilted to extinguish the blaze. When this actually happened, the water helped to complete the damage which the flames had overlooked.

By unwritten agreement, the north side of Front Street was regarded as "respectable." Here, besides Wright's and Beebe's two hotels, Tom O'Keefe's blacksmith shop, the retail stores and Dieter's Barber Shop, were the better-class saloons—notably the Long Branch, named for the New Jersey resort which half-owner Will Harris had visited in youth, and Peter Beatty's and Jim "Dog" Kelley's neighboring Alhambra.

On the South Side, where, it was generally agreed, "anything goes," were the less reputable but equally popular establishments: the Lady Gay Dance Hall and Saloon, which presented nightly entertainment; the Comique Theater (pronounced "Commi-kew" in Dodge), named after Harrigan and Hart's theater in New York, which presented traveling stock shows and vaudeville; and Rowdy Kate Lowe's notorious Green Front Saloon. While citizens of standing patronized the North Side places of amusement, at least until their wives had gone to bed, the South Side with its uninhibited and raucous revelry was the ultimate attraction. As one Dodgeite observed, "It was only a few steps from the Long Branch to the Lady Gay, but every step was paved with bad intentions."

All the dance halls and saloons provided gambling. Hundreds, sometimes thousands, of dollars passed across the gaming tables. For the town was still Buffalo City despite its change of name, and buffalo money was the key to its vitality. From 1872 to 1874, two million hides were shipped from Dodge via the Santa Fe, along with three million pounds of meat. Charlie Rath, according to his partner, "bought and sold more than a million buffalo hides, and tens of thousands of buffalo robes, and hundreds of cars

of buffalo meat, both dried and fresh, besides several
carloads of buffalo tongues."

Brick Bond, now employing fifteen skinners,
claimed to have shot more buffalo than any man
alive, although the newly established Dodge City
Times reported that "the best record is that of Tom
Nixon who killed 120 at one stand in 40 minutes with
a total of 2173 buffaloes in nine months." During the
last big season, beginning in 1876, Brick Bond killed
5855 buffalo for an extraordinary average of 197 a
day. In retribution, Bond was permanently deafened
by the ceaseless explosions of his Sharps Big Fifty
rifle.

In like proportion, as the herds diminished, the
Plainsmen and freighters continued to bring in the
skeletons and bones for shipment to the manufactur-
ers of fertilizer. The comedian Eddie Foy, arriving
by the Santa Fe with his partner for an engagement
at the Comique Theater, saw from the windows of
the car "an enormous pile of bones beside the track
that must have been twenty-five feet high and a
hundred feet long. The sight suggested to our minds
that they might be killing people in Dodge City
faster than they could bury them." Foy's conclusion
was right to the degree that homicidal shootings in
that lawless hunter's paradise were becoming an
everyday affair.

North of the town was a treeless bluff which the

city shortly branded "Boot Hill." The story went
that two cowboys, camping on the elevation overnight, engaged in a quarrel in which one had shot
the other. The killer fled, and the corpse of the unknown victim was discovered the next morning and
buried without ceremony with his boots on. The knoll
became the graveyard for many ill-starred victims of
Dodge City violence, while the name Boot Hill was
shortly applied to the cemeteries of other Kansas
cowtowns. Bob Wright estimated that in Dodge's first
year as a city some twenty-three to twenty-five men
were shot and buried on Boot Hill, though nobody
kept official records of the killings.

With no law-enforcement body nearer than Hays
City, ninety miles north of Dodge, the matter of
curbing the suicidal instincts of its trigger-happy
population fell upon the citizens—a dangerous burden
in civilian hands. In 1873 the secret Society of Vigilantes was organized, headed by buffalo hunter Tom
Nixon. It had only one fault, common to vigilante
groups throughout the history of the West. Its members were often as lawless and unprincipled as those
they sought to regulate.

When the commander at Fort Dodge sent his ser-
vant into town to pick up some merchandise, two of
the vigilantes thought it a playful joke to steal his
gig. The black man rushed out, and tried to intervene. The vigilantes shot him dead. When word of
the killing reached the commander, he wired the

governor of Kansas for permission to enter Dodge to arrest and punish the offenders. Permission was naturally granted.

Hearing of Colonel Dodge's planned invasion, Nixon assembled his fifty armed vigilantes, and sent word to the commander that his men would shoot any bluecoat trying to march upon the city. Colonel Dodge brushed the threat aside, and in true movie tradition the U. S. Cavalry, trumpets blowing and flags streaming in the wind, swept into Dodge a few paces behind the fleeing defenders. The culprits were nabbed and hauled back to the fort for trial, and the word "vigilante" was seldom heard in Dodge again.

But the need for some sort of law-enforcement body was apparent. In 1873 Ford County was organized, with Dodge the county seat, and Charlie Bassett was appointed sheriff. Policing the streets of Dodge, however, was not part of Charlie's duties. Concerned citizens headed by Bob Wright got together and raised enough money to hire a city marshal. The offices of sheriff and marshal, while they sometimes called for cooperation in emergencies, were by no means similar. The sheriff's authority covered a wide area of which the city was a part; the marshal's duties were generally confined to Dodge alone.

In choosing its first marshal, Dodge followed the pattern and experience of earlier frontier towns like

Abilene and Wichita. A man's principles and past were unimportant. But his reputation with a six-gun was. Could he outdraw his probable opponents? How many men had he killed in gunfights? Was he as tough as or tougher than the professional gambler, gunman, and the trigger-happy Texas cowboys who were coming to the city in increasing numbers?

Among the local talent present was young Billy Brooks, former marshal of Newton, who had already distinguished himself in Dodge by shooting and killing an agent of the Santa Fe. Brooks was happy to wear the badge and make his homicidal instinct legal. In the first thirty days of holding office, Billy reportedly killed or wounded fifteen men. Four brothers of one of the victims came to town to seek revenge. Learning of their approach, Brooks stood in the center of Front Street, a revolver in each hand. As the quartet appeared he fired four shots in lightning-quick succession before the others had a chance to draw. When the smoke cleared, four men lay dead as tombstones on the street.

A quarrel over a dance-hall girl named Lizzie Palmer put an end to Brooks' career in Dodge. The marshal's rival for Lizzie's affections was young Kirk Jordan, record-breaking buffalo hunter. Jordan came looking for Billy one afternoon, and the two approached each other warily on Front Street. Suddenly, from a curious yellow streak that sometimes affected professional gunmen, Billy's nerve gave out.

He ducked behind one of the water-filled barrels on the sidewalk just as Jordan opened fire.

According to Josiah Mooar, who witnessed the incident, the riddled barrel "went boogle, boogle, boogle, drenching Billy to the skin." Thinking he had killed the marshal, Jordan rode contentedly away. But though Kirk had been cheated of his revenge, Billy Brooks, in Dodge's opinion, was as good as dead. Bob Wright gave Billy just time enough to dry out and then put him on the next train going east, echoing the town's opinion of "Good riddance!"

Brooks was succeeded by Billy Rivers, whose term of office was even shorter. If the sequence of names —Brooks, Rivers, and later Bridges—suggests the liquidlike flowing of marshals in and out of Dodge those early years, the impression is correct. Few could stand up to that toughening town, which was rapidly changing from Buffalo City to Cowboy Capital of the West. In increasing numbers the herds were coming up the Chisholm Trail and later the Texas Trail to Dodge in preference to the more distant terminals of Abilene and Wichita.

Late in 1873 Bob Wright and another leading citizen, Alonzo "Ab" Webster, proprietor of the Alamo Saloon, built a wooden toll bridge across the Arkansas to allow the herds to reach the grazing grounds above the city. The Santa Fe began constructing yards and pens for cattle awaiting shipment to the East. A year later, after dusk, the prai-

ries around Dodge were picturesquely lit by the
fires of forty or fifty cowmen's camps, while Dodge
itself was still more picturesquely taken over by the
hordes of cowboys swarming into town to find an
outlet for their pent-up spirits and the four to six
months' wages in their pockets.

By 1875 Dodge realized, with a sort of joyous
trepidation, that it was about to become the leading
cattle town of Kansas and the great Southwest. It
would have to shape up to the image. In late Decem-
ber, a five-man city council comprising leading citizens met to appoint Peter L. Beatty, co-owner with
Jim "Dog" Kelley of the Alhambra, provisional mayor
until formal elections could be held. The council also
passed certain measures "relating to the licensing of
dram shops, defining misdemeanors and providing
punishments for same."

Under the new laws nobody could ride a horse
into a dance hall or saloon. Guns could not be carried on the streets, but had to be checked in racks
provided in such central places as the Wright House
and the Long Branch; they could not be returned
to anyone who was obviously intoxicated. All three
measures—and there were others, too—were regarded as outrageous violations of one's civil rights.
A cowboy or hunter felt naked without his guns and
sometimes lost without his pony drinking with him
at the bar. As for drunkenness, why should a hard-
working hunter or cowboy be denied the right to

clear his throat of prairie dust with plenty of good bourbon?

In the absence of a city jail, a sixteen-foot well was dug on the Plaza, into which were pitched offending citizens or visitors, generally obstreperous drunks. Given time to dry out in the well, they were resurrected when they appeared sober, and allowed to return to their former drinking haunts. Known as Dodge City's "Keeley cure," it did not reform the alcoholic but it provided a respite for the rest of the community.

The dance halls and saloons, and above all the gambling parlors, were allowed to run at full tilt. They were indisputable business assets to the city, supplying needed income. And above all they provided a strong attraction to the cattlemen who were starting to recognize Dodge City as the foremost shipping center of the Santa Fe. Even the unsavory patrons of these places—the gamblers, gunmen, tinhorn shysters, and scarlet women—helped to keep the gambling tables going, the wheels spinning, the liquor pouring, and the girls in pocket money. Was the city supposed to eliminate such blessings? "Why shoot Santa Claus?" was the accepted answer.

Yet the businessmen of Front Street, the proprietors of the places of entertainment, were concerned about their property and the safety of their patrons. The ban on carrying weapons was difficult to enforce, easy to evade. Alcohol, cards, and guns were a perilous mixture. More than mere laws were needed to curb the violence.

In the first free vote for mayor, P. L. Beatty declined the nomination and George Hoover was elected on the law-and-order ticket. In choosing a city marshal Hoover had his pick of experienced gun fighters in the city: Billy Tilghman, Bat and Ed Masterson, the Cherokee half-breed Neal Brown, Tom Nixon, and Mysterious Dave Mather. But he settled for Lawrence E. Deger, a German-American with political connections. The obese, gregarious Deger was popular enough and all right as a figurehead, but hardly a fast man with a gun. To provide the actual skill and muscle, Hoover selected as chief deputy a notorious gunman named Jack Allen.

In spite of his formidable reputation, Allen lasted no longer than most of his predecessors. The first trail gang to hit the city in the spring of 1876, heralding Dodge's peak year as a cattle town, broke every ordinance in the book. Allen sought refuge in the railroad depot, leaving the cowboys free to "hurrah" the town—a term applied to unrestrained gunplay in the streets, shooting out lamps and windows in the saloons, lassoing the dance-hall girls, and ravaging the city like a wartime army on the loose. From his place of hiding Allen decided he had had enough. The next morning he left town.

Mayor Hoover thought the situation over. He had known young Wyatt Earp as an expert buffalo hunter in the early days of Dodge, a sure shot with a rifle or revolver, and had heard of his brief success as marshal of both Wichita and Ellsworth. He telegraphed Wyatt, offering him the position of assistant city marshal, thereby launching the era of the great peace officers of Dodge—not only of Dodge, in fact, but of the whole Southwest, of which Dodge City had become the honorary capital.

4

Cattle Drives and Drovers

Early in the spring we round up the dogies,
Mark and brand and bob off their tails;
Round up our horses, load up the chuck wagon,
Then throw the dogies upon the trail.
Trail Song of the Texas Herder

If the buffalo built Dodge City in the first place, it
was the Texas Longhorns that made it the Queen of
the Cowtowns. For almost a decade they had been
coming up the Chisholm Trail from assembly points
near San Antonio, first to the railhead at Abilene,
where they reached their peak in numbers in 1872,
then taking westward cutoffs to Hays and Ellsworth
as the railroad reached those towns, and finally via
the Chisholm and Western Trails to Dodge.

Bred in the wild from Spanish cattle, the Longhorns were a unique and extraordinary breed. With
widespread, pointed horns giving them their name,
they weighed at maturity from a thousand to sixteen
hundred pounds. Yet in spite of the cumbersome

weight, they were fleet and fierce, and as unpredict-
able as any creature of the wild. J. Frank Dobie, an
authority on the American Southwest, reported that
"a herd of full-grown Texas steers might appear to
a stranger seeing them for the first time as a parody
of their kind."

> But however they appeared, with their steel hoofs,
> their long legs, their staglike muscles, their thick
> skins, their powerful horns, they could walk the rough-
> est ground, cross the widest deserts, climb the highest
> mountains, swim the widest rivers, fight off the
> fiercest band of wolves, endure hunger, cold, thirst
> and punishment as few beasts of the earth have
> ever shown themselves capable of enduring. On the
> prairies they could run like antelopes; in the thickets
> of thorn and tangle they could break their way with
> the agility of panthers. They could rustle in drought
> or snow, smell out pasturage leagues away, live like
> true captains of their own souls and bodies.
>
> They were the cow brutes for the open range,
> the cattle of the hour. They suited the wide, un-
> tamed land and the men that ranged it.

As early as 1872 D. Wilburn "Doc" Barton, then
only nineteen but destined to become one of the
famous cowmen of the West, brought a herd of two
thousand Longhorns up to Dodge. Finding the city
ill prepared to handle such a charge, with no pens
yet erected by the railroad, he pushed on to a railhead farther north. In the next two years, after several acres of yards had been installed, the cattle con-

tinued to come in encouraging numbers; but it was
not until 1875, when more than 180,000 Longhorns
blanketed the range lands around Dodge, that the
city really hit its stride as a predominantly cattle
town.

By then it was better prepared for the invasion,
not only with corrals and shipping pens, but with the
well-established gambling houses, dance halls, and
saloons, tested for their durability by the hunters.
Nevertheless the arrival of the Texas cowboys—from
several hundred to the later bands of several thousand in a single night—was a challenge to the town's
stability. With rebel yells and blazing guns they galloped into town as if they owned it. Their arrogance and irrepressible high spirits put the city's
nerves on edge. Wrote cowtown chronicler Stuart
Lake:

> Cowboys pre-empted the dance-hall belles, broke
> up variety shows, rode their ponies on the sidewalks
> and into the saloons, held up gambling games and
> openly spent their pilfered coin on further hilarity;
> shot the windows out of stores, the lights out of
> places of amusement and the same out of individuals
> who protested. Texas men bragged that they in-
> tended to run the town and welcomed any chance
> to prove it.

With hordes of buffalo hunters, gunmen, gamblers,
and soldiers from the fort already in the city, the
mixture was explosive. If no other reason for fric-

tion existed, the Texans despised these Northerners; they had been enemies in the recent War Between the States. In turn, the more renegade elements of the town—the crooked gamblers, thieves, and sometimes dance-hall girls—regarded the cowboy as easy pickings, a dupe to be relieved of any money he possessed. Such places as the Lone Star Dance Hall and Saloon, named of course for Texas, was a trap for the cowboy's pride and gullibility.

Yet in spite of the trouble they often brought, the Texas cowboys (they were called "herders" then, or "cowpokes" and "cowpunchers") became in time essential, although transient, citizens of Dodge. They helped to shape the city's character and life and place in Western history. To understand the nature of the man himself, and the very real contribution he made, one must understand a bit about his life upon the range.

The drives started from Texas in the early spring, after the annual roundup of the cattle that had fattened through the winter's grazing, and the branding of the new calves added to the herd. As many as two to three thousand head might constitute an average drive, accompanied by thirty cowboys. Each had a string of half a dozen ponies, comprising the *remuda,* or supply of horses provided by the owner. The thousand miles from southern Texas up to Dodge, with the cattle moving at twelve to fifteen miles a day, might take ten weeks or more.

The cowboy's pay averaged forty dollars a month, with top herders sometimes getting fifty dollars. This gave him a stake of a hundred to a hundred and fifty dollars when he reached his destination. The figure might vary with the generosity of the owner. Some cowboys arrived in Dodge with as much as three hundred dollars in their pockets, of which they had rarely a penny left when they departed.

It was far from easy money. Up before dawn, and twelve to fourteen hours in the saddle, living off beans and beef and grease from the chuck wagon following the herd. They rode through alternate heat and cold, blizzards and drought, with the scarlet kerchiefs around their necks raised as masks against the driving wind and sand. Strays had to be chased and rounded up; rivers had to be forded, with steers often floundering in quicksand; detours had to be made when an expected water hole was not found. There was no shelter or bedding other than the cowboy's saddle blanket, which contained his scanty personal belongings.

At night the herd was bedded down, the horses corralled, and night watches were scheduled, the men working in shifts of two to four hours. The night herders, making their rounds in opposite directions so that they could meet and check with one another, relieved the monotony by singing to the dormant cattle to keep them quiet—avoiding the livelier tunes and sticking to hymns and ballads which the Longhorns seemed to find more soothing. Among the wealth of anonymous prairie verse appears the quatrain:

> What keeps the herd from running,
> Stampeding far and wide?
> The cowboy's long low whistle,
> And singing by their side.

Stampedes were the real and present danger of the cattle drive, occurring generally at night. Any sudden noise—the snapping of a stick, a coyote's yowl, a clap of thunder—could send the animals into precipitous flight. A cowboy might light a cigarette; the wind would catch a spark and the spark would settle on a steer. In seconds the silent prairie became alive with thundering hoofs as the herd took off across the Plains. "Sometimes," noted cowboy Andy Adams, "the friction of the speeding cattle caused weird blue flashes to quiver at the tips of their long horns."

Instantly aroused and in the saddle, the cowboys would take off in a race to overtake the lead steer. With shouts and pistol fire they would force the leading steer to turn, tracing a wide arc, and the rest would follow until the front end of the column met the tail. Then the whole herd became a vast and milling circle whirling around like a wheel until it slowed down from exhaustion.

In the initial stages of a stampede the cattle were

uncontrollable; every man had to look out for himself. "It was beef against horseflesh," a veteran trail driver said, "with the odds on beef for the first few hundred yards." Teddy Blue, a veteran ranchman, recounted one of the many tragic accidents in such emergencies. Reporting on one man missing after a storm and cattle stampede, Blue recorded:

> We went back to look for him, and we found him among the prairie dog holes, beside his horse. The horse's ribs was scraped bare of hide, and all the rest of horse and man was mashed into the ground flat as a pancake. The only thing you could recognize was the handle of his six-shooter.

There was, too, the peril of prairie fires caused by lightning; later winter blizzards that could freeze to death both men and cattle; and the constant threat of Indian attacks, especially between the Texas border and the Arkansas. Marauding bands would follow the drive at a cautious distance. Lurking outside the camp at night, they would wait for a chance to surreptitiously stampede the herd, then capture any strays that became separated in the melee. Or they might openly intercept a drive out of need for beef and other food. The trail boss who saw himself badly outnumbered would be forced to turn over a portion of his cattle, sometimes as much as 10 percent, to save the herd.

There was little relaxation or amusement on the trail. Drinking was not allowed, and gambling was no temptation since the drovers took the sensible precaution of not paying their men until they reached their destination. Singing around the fire at night, accompanied by a guitar, was common, with the ribald ditty often followed by a sacred hymn. Another popular diversion was reading aloud the labels from discarded food cans, such as recipes for Boston baked beans, or directions for preparing certain brands of coffee, or for using other brands of baking powder. Memorized and put to invented or familiar tunes, these later might be crooned to the music-loving cows at night.

And there was always the practical joker to enliven things. Griping about chuck-wagon food was as common as in an army mess. But one dared not go too far; the cook was too important to offend. One chronic complainer was warned by the boss, "Cut it out! One more word outa you, and you're headin' back to Texas." Overhearing this, a camp wag saw a means of putting his fellow herder on the spot. That night in the chuck line he surreptitiously slipped a buffalo chip on his companion's plate in place of the expected steak. After one mouthful the outraged victim exploded: "This tastes like cow dung!" Then, recalling his boss's warning, quickly added, "But it's delicious!"

Every trail herd had its scout to ride ahead, check the range for grass and water, and report on the level of rivers to be forded. In this capacity, one Tommy

Lovell invented a spur-of-the-moment diversion. Approaching an unfamiliar Kansas river, he found it wide but only several inches deep, with the water too muddy to see the bottom.

Lovell rode back and reported on the river to his fellow herders. It was six to ten feet deep, he warned. He suggested that he and the cook ride ahead and float the chuck wagon across, to get that first chore over with. Then the others, when they reached the bank, could swim their horses over, with the water-borne cattle flanked between them.

The procedure was followed. Tommy and the cook raced ahead, easily rolled the wagon across, then waited on the farther bank for the cowboys to arrive. Soon twenty or more herders reached the bank, stripped to their spurs, then whooped and shouted to the cattle as they plunged their horses bravely into the forbidding river. It was an unforgettable spectacle, as Tommy later told it every time he had the chance—a score of naked cowboys plunging bravely into the forbidding water, whooping and gesturing at the steers; then suddenly growing scarlet with chagrin as they rode their ponies across a river that barely covered the horses' hoofs, accompanied by cattle as bewildered by the farce as were their masters.

George Duffield, a cowboy accompanying a herd of Longhorns north from San Antonio, is one of the few who kept a diary of a Texas cattle drive. Some typical excerpts are revealing:

> *May 1. Big Stampede. Lost 200 head of cattle.*
> *May 2. Spent all day hunting and found but 20 Head. It has been Raining for three days. These are dark days for me.*
> *May 3. Day spent in hunting Cattle. Hard rain and wind. Lots of trouble.*

Some later entries, on and after crossing the Brazos River:

> *May 14. Swam our cattle & Horses & built Raft & Rafted our provisions & blankets etc. over. Swam river with rope & then hauled wagon over. Lost Most of our Kitchen furniture such as camp Kettles Coffee Pots Cups Plates Canteens &c*
> *May 15. It does nothing but rain. Got all our traps together that was not lost & thought we were ready for off. Dark rainy night. Cattle all left us & in morning not one Beef to be seen.*
> *May 16. Hunt Beeves is the word—all Hands discouraged & are determined to quit. 200 Beeves out & nothing to eat.*

Later, after one man drowned in a river crossing, another stampede, two men lost in a rain and wind storm, and no food for sixty hours, this entry:

> *June 17. 15 Indians came to Herd & tried to take some Beeves. Would not let them. Had a big muss. One drew his Knife & I my Revolver. Made them leave but fear they have gone for others.*

And finally, on reaching the Arkansas River west of Dodge:

> *June 27. My Back is Blistered badly from exposure while in the River & I with two others are suffering very much. I was attacked by a Beefe in the River & had a very narrow escape from being hurt by Diving.*

Others reported death lurking on the prairies, sometimes by lightning, sometimes from trampling by stampeding cattle, often by a running horse catching his hoof in a prairie-dog hole and inflicting the rider with a broken neck. The victim was buried where he fell, wrapped in his saddle blanket; the trail boss read a service from the Bible; and the grave was covered with round, smooth rocks, with no wood available for a marker.

Little wonder, then—after three months on the trail, through heat, dust, rain, wind, rivers, Indians, cattle rustlers, overturned chuck wagons, dwindling rations, and stampedes—when the cowboy finally heard the whistle of a train and saw the dingy false-front buildings of Dodge City, he broke into a rebel yell. No ivory-towered capital of palaces and kings, such as are seen in prairie mirages, ever seemed more welcome than that sprawling, shabby city on the Plains.

The arriving herds were preceded by their owner-ranchers and by buyers and speculators from the Midwestern cities and the East. They holed up at Deacon Cox's new Dodge House or Bob Wright's

hotel and spent their waiting afternoons at the Long
Branch or the Alhambra, engaging in preliminary
bickering on the forthcoming sale. They were in no
hurry. For every owner this was the only trail drive
of the year, and since the cattle were sold by weight
it was well to let them graze for a while on the
neighboring prairies. One shrewd operator resorted
to force-feeding his herd on salt before a sale, then
allowing them to quench their thirst on quart after
quart of water, adding eight pounds of weight with
every gallon.

As the herds arrived in Dodge, the prairies blos-
somed with a score of cattle camps. Long before
nightfall, the cowboys hastened to the magic city,
pockets bulging with their wages, bottled-up spirits
pressured to the breaking point from long days on
the trail.

But the initial goal was not the dens of dissipa-
tion. The average cowhand headed first for Dieter's
barber shop for a haircut and a shave. Then to
Wright & Beverley's for the personal accouterments
so dear to the heart of every cowboy: a new Stetson
from Philadelphia, new Mexican boots with silver
stars around the top—for the star was the Texan's
favorite, most ubiquitous adornment; then perhaps
an embroidered vest and surely a new set of jingling
spurs, the latter as much a cowboy's trademark as
the star. The sound of the spurs as he trod the
wooden sidewalks reassured the Texan of his identity

and relieved his sense of loneliness in an unfamiliar town.

Andy Adams, a onetime Texas cowboy who, in his youthful twenties, made almost yearly drives to Dodge, has left an accurate account of life upon the range. He also described the cowboys' arrival and trail-end festivities at Dodge in his book, *The Log of a Cowboy.*

Andy's account of a trail-end evening in Dodge City follows the classic cowboy formula, neither underplayed nor overglamorized. First, bathed and shaved, the men had drinks and dinner at Delmonico's or the Wright House, followed by a sampling of the dance halls and the gambling saloons, where most of the company parted with their earnings. Next, the inevitable fistfight at the bar, followed by forcible ejection at the hands of the strong-armed bouncer. And finally an angry return to the saloon with reinforcements to obtain revenge. This consisted of pistol-whipping the bouncer, shooting out the lights, and generally wrecking the establishment, and was followed by a galloping retreat down Front Street with the more unruly citizens taking pot shots at them on the general principle that fleeing cowboys were legitimate, inviting targets on the streets of Dodge.

Texas owners and drovers rarely tried to curb the wild exuberance of their men. The chance to break loose and hurrah the city was part of their recompense for all the stringencies and self-denials of the trail. If the cowboys landed in jail, the owners bailed them out, for loyalty within the clan was absolute. Nor were owners and drovers themselves averse to a little hell-raising, gambling, and drinking with the men. In the cattle towns, every man was equal, and the Texans were more equal than their Northern counterparts.

In fact, the big-time cattle barons were often as much of a problem in Dodge as the obstreperous cowboys they employed. Abel "Shanghai" Pierce was a good (or bad) example—250 pounds of New England Yankee converted by circumstance and inclination to a typical Southwest cattle rancher. Fellow Texans idolized him, sheriffs and marshals were fearful of his bulk and influential wealth. When Shanghai got drunk and resorted to his favorite amusement of shooting the ornaments off Front Street buildings, the only tactic was to lure him back to the saloon for free drinks, ply him with liquor till he passed out, and then remove his guns and carry him to bed.

Usually one night on the town was enough to exhaust the average cowboy's pay, though the herders might be camping on the prairie for a week or more until the cattle were disposed of. In return for his lost wages the Texan had a king-size headache but a host of cherished memories, with stories aplenty to entertain his comrades in the winter months to come.

The final business before breaking camp was, of course, the sale of the herd. While an accurate counting of heads and estimation of weight might be insisted on by the appraiser, a popular method was known as "cutting on the run." If a buyer wanted a thousand head, the seller's herd was driven past a given point with all involved professing to keep count. As Andy Adams heard it described by Shanghai Pierce:

> I was selling a thousand beef steers one time to some Yankee contractors, and they had agreed to take a running cut. Well, my foreman and I were counting the cattle as they came between us. I lost count several times but kept on guessing and the cattle kept on coming like a whirlwind; and when I thought about nine hundred had passed us, I cut them off and sang out, "Just an even thousand, by gatlins! What do you make it, Bill?"
>
> "Just an even thousand, Colonel," replied my foreman.
>
> Of course the contractors were counting at the same time, and didn't like to admit they couldn't count a thousand cattle as fast as we, so they accepted and paid for them. They grazed the cattle outside that night, but the next day, when they cut them into car lots to be shipped, they were a hundred and eighteen short. They wanted me to make good the difference, but shucks! I wasn't responsible if their outfit had lost some cattle overnight.

With the herd cut to the buyer's order, the cattle were driven up planks to the slatted cars of the eastbound Santa Fe train. That wound up work for most of the hands, but a few went along with the cattle cars to poke at the steers and keep them from lying down (since a prostrate animal took up needed space), using a wooden prod like a billiard cue. Hence the names cowpuncher and cowpoke, terms that later became confused with the herd-riding hands or cowboys.

By 1876, when the quarantine line against Texas fever was moved farther west, Dodge experienced its first big year as a leading cattle center of the Southwest. Jack Potter, who that year blazed the Western, or Dodge City, Trail, reported that "we were driving tens of thousands of Longhorn cattle up this trail from the breeding grounds of Texas. With a crew of cowboys and a wrangler [horse tender] to handle our remuda, we poked along some ten to twelve miles a day, with thousands of Longhorns always headed, every step of the way, straight toward the shipping pens of Dodge City, notorious 'cowboy capital of the world.' "

Dodge by that time was certainly notorious, and with the growing influx of Texas cowboys things were getting out of hand. It was early that spring that Mayor Hoover felt the need for adding muscle to his law-enforcement body and sent to Wichita for Wyatt Earp.

5

The Men Behind the Badge

And the sheriff he came too, he came too;
Yes, the sheriff he came too, he came too;
Yes, the sheriff he came too, with his men all dressed
   in blue,
Lord, they were a bloody crew, damn their eyes!
                              Song of Sam Hall

That Dodge City in its heyday was a lawless, trigger-happy town is a popular legend of the West. It is also the truth. Perhaps the truth has been magnified in films and fiction. But when, at the end of a cattle drive, hundreds of rambunctious cowboys were turned loose on Front Street with no outlet for their pent-up spirits beyond drinking, gambling, and fighting, it was reasonable to expect the worst. Add to this volatile population the itinerant gamblers, outlaws, and shady promoters protecting their interests with a fast gun, and the mixture was explosive.

The arrival in Dodge of Wyatt Earp in May 1876 marked the beginning of an era in that city's efforts to keep law and order within bounds—a new era, for that matter, in the struggle to bring law to the entire West. This is not giving Earp himself undue importance. His action-packed career has often been exaggerated, by himself as well as others. But as assistant marshal under Larry Deger he topped a long list of marshals and sheriffs that were outstanding in the West: Wyatt, Virgil, and Morgan Earp; Bat Masterson and his brothers Jim and Ed; Charlie Bassett, Billy Tilghman, Mysterious Dave Mather and Ham Bell, to name a few.

They were difficult characters to pigeonhole. It was sometimes uncertain just which side they represented, lawlessness or law and order, and often they represented both. Many of them came from other cowtowns that had passed their peak—such as Abilene, where Wild Bill Hickok reigned as both incorrigible bully and respected lawman; Wichita and Ellsworth, where Wyatt Earp briefly wore a badge; Hays and Newton, where Jack Bridges and Billy Brooks, respectively, started their careers.

Appointments to office were often based on urgent necessity rather than on a careful canvassing of recruits, with on-the-spot selections made in moments of emergency. The only qualification was skill in handling a gun; there was no time or inclination to examine a man's past or principles. Thus Wyatt

Earp was brought to the side of the law during a gunfight in Ellsworth in August 1873. As an innocent bystander Earp witnessed the shooting of Sheriff C. B. Whitney by the notorious gunman Billy Thompson and his brother Ben.

Mayor Jim Miller also witnessed the killing, and as his deputy sheriffs fled the scene he spotted Earp on the sidelines, knew of his reputation as a marksman, and pleaded with Wyatt to intervene.

"It's none of my business," Wyatt said.

"I'll make it your business," Miller told him, handing him a badge. "You're marshal of Ellsworth. Go get Thompson!"

Earp was a man who instinctively responded to a crisis. While Billy had done the shooting, Ben was keeping the crowd at bay to allow his brother to escape, thus becoming an accessory to the crime. Wyatt approached Ben with his fingers close to his holsters and called on the gunman to surrender. Ben eyed the marshal critically, sizing up his chances. Then, surprisingly, he grinned and dropped his gun. "I didn't want to die just then," he later told Bat Masterson, "and I had a hunch I would if Wyatt went after his guns."

While Billy made good his escape, Ben Thompson was tried for murder and fined twenty-five dollars for disturbing the peace. Disgusted at the decision, Wyatt turned in the badge, which he had worn for just an hour.

"If Ellsworth figures marshals at twenty-five dollars a head," he said, "it isn't big enough for me." He may have been right.

"Wyatt Earp's short journey across the Ellsworth plaza under the muzzle of Ben Thompson's shotgun established for all time his preeminence among gunfighters of the West," wrote Earp's biographer Stuart Lake, adding that the episode had generally been ignored by history.

The following spring Earp arrived in Dodge as assistant marshal under Larry Deger. The appendage of "assistant" was a sop to Deger's pride. Actually Earp was paid more than his boss—$250 a month, which was high for such a post—and was allowed to pick his own deputies, Neal Brown and Joe Mason, at seventy-five dollars a month each.

Exaggerated and belittled, twisted by fiction and sometimes lost in legend, Wyatt Earp's character and career have been variously represented. While he may not always have acted with the noblest of motives, he was nonetheless the prototype of the Western lawman.

For one thing he looked the part: six feet tall, lean and muscular, clear-cut features with blue eyes that were frank but penetrating, light brown hair, and a determined, slightly jutting chin. He carried himself with the ease and grace of an athlete, and dressed conservatively in black cowboy boots, black trousers, white shirt, and black wide-brimmed hat.

He never drank, was quiet and reserved in boisterous company, and was gentle of manner when he chose to be.

But his trigger-sharp quickness with a gun was legendary. Bat Masterson, who had met Wyatt on the Salt Fork of the Arkansas in 1872, declared that the latter's speed and skill with a Colt forty-five made even the most talented gunmen, such as the Thompsons and Clay Allison, reluctant to face up to him. On top of that was unshakable courage. The West, according to Masterson, "knew no braver man than Wyatt Earp. He was destitute of fear . . . a loyal friend, but a dangerous enemy."

Also, Wyatt Earp approached his duties with a definite philosophy and code of conduct. His methods were so successful that others were prompted to follow his example. Briefly his rules were:

1. Use tact and reason before resorting to gunplay. A man ceases to be dangerous if you can keep him talking.

2. If you have to use your guns, take your time, keep cool, be certain of your aim. The man who shoots first, and hastily, is not necessarily the winner.

3. If you have to shoot, then shoot to maim, not kill. (As Wyatt said on his first appointment as city marshal, "I was hired to stop the killing, not to add to it.")

With regard to the third precept, it is significant that Dodge's marshals and sheriffs were responsible for very few killings in the city, though legend boasts of scores of victims. Wyatt Earp killed only one man on the streets of Dodge, though he wounded others in the line of duty. Bat Masterson, credited with twenty-three killings, was responsible for only one in Dodge. Billy Tilghman, Charlie Bassett, Larry Deger, and Ed Masterson had bloodless records.

Most of the gunfights in Dodge resulted from petty feuds or personal grudges, or insults to the sensitive pride of overarrogant Texans. It was Wyatt's policy simply to "take the starch out" of offending cowboys. This he did chiefly by "buffaloing" the miscreant, or knocking him unconscious with the heavy barrel of his forty-five. A cowboy thus subdued remained subdued; he was chastened or "destarched" by the very thought that the marshal had not seen fit to fire his guns.

Nor was Earp reluctant to use his fists in place of firearms. Each trail herd had its bare-fisted, rough-and-tumble champion among the cowboys. One two-hundred-pounder used his spurs as well as fists to gouge an opponent once he got him down. Egged on by his mates, he challenged Wyatt to drop his guns and fight him on the street with no holds barred. The fight was over before the cowboy knew it. Wyatt hit him three times, once in the jaw, then in the stomach, then in the jaw again—leaving him to be carried off by his supporters.

Bat Masterson recalls a doubleheader that took place shortly afterward. The first bout was with a hulking cowhand, hailed as the champion of Texas. The battle lasted twenty minutes, during which Earp pounded the giant into pulp but was himself severely bruised and bloodied. As Wyatt glanced over the rest of the Texans, asking: "Anybody else want trouble?" Masterson cautioned him to rest on his laurels. "No," said Wyatt, "either I run this town or I don't." The next man to step into the ring was punched into temporary imbecility. Wyatt looked around for yet another challenger; none stepped forth.

It was under Wyatt Earp's three terms as marshal that certain procedures were established for policing Dodge. A hypothetical Dead Line was established down the center of the Plaza. North of that line no guns could be fired or carried on the street. South of the line, there was practically no law whatever, short of murder. If revelers wanted to engage in gunplay, rough up one another, or drink themselves to death, the South Side was the place to do it. A permanent jail was also erected, a massive square box of planks and bars, to replace the sixteen-foot well as a repository for offenders.

Since there were no taxes to support the marshal and his deputies, and since saloonkeepers, gamblers, and scarlet ladies of the town regarded licensing as an infringement of their freedom, a system of monthly "fines" was established—five dollars a month for gamblers, ten dollars for prostitutes, fifty dollars for wholesale liquor dealers. It came to the same thing as licensing or taxing, but it was regarded as "more democratic." To provide some further income for the marshal and his deputies, $2.50 bonuses were offered for each "live" arrest, with a ten-dollar bounty for apprehending dangerous criminals.

William B. Masterson himself was another gunfighter who was enlisted on the side of law by chance. After the affair with the railroad foreman Ritter, when the Masterson brothers forcibly collected their back wages for working on the Santa Fe, Ed Masterson stayed on to become assistant marshal in Dodge, while Bat drifted in and out of town. In Sweetwater, Texas, Bat was shot in the hip in a gunfight over a local siren and ever after limped with a cane. He reportedly used the cane to crack the heads of his opponents, thereby gaining the nickname "Bat." A more likely explanation is that the pseudonym came from a shortening of his middle name, Bartholomew.

Bat, now twenty-three years old, was back in Dodge in June 1877, when the town was crowded with rambunctious trail hands. Marshal Deger, trying to keep order, arrested a clownish cowboy named Bobby Gill, who was challenging his authority. Bobby put up a scuffle on being led toward the jail, and the marshal booted him in the rear. Bat

Masterson happened to be standing by, and this example of "police brutality" offended his sensibilities. He wrapped an arm around the marshal's neck and held on until Bobby could escape.

Deger's deputies, except for Ed Masterson, hurried to the marshal's aid. Bat was pistol-whipped, generally roughed up and bloodied, and propelled toward the city jail. The Dodge City *Times* reported:

> Bat Masterson seemed possessed of extraordinary strength, and every inch of the way was closely contested, but the city dungeon was reached at last, and in he went. Had he got hold of his gun, before going in, there would have been a general killing.

Bat's older brother Ed, whose job as assistant marshal had put him in a difficult position, later arrested Bobby Gill and threw him in the jail with Bat. There was nothing he could do for Bat himself.

The strange consequence of Bat Masterson's tangle with the law was that after the trial Mayor Jim Kelley revoked Bat's fine and persuaded him to serve as deputy under Charlie Bassett, sheriff of Ford County. Although the sheriff and the city marshal sometimes aided one another, it didn't happen this time. Bat emerged from jail wearing a sheriff's badge, and at once set his sights for the marshal who had pistol-whipped him. Within a month the *Times* reported that Deger had resigned his position "at the request of Under Sheriff Masterson."

When Wyatt Earp returned to Dodge after a winter's absence, he and Bat renewed their acquaintance, remaining friends for life. Masterson was well liked in the city but was quite the opposite in character of Wyatt Earp. Genial and gregarious, he much preferred drinking and gambling to the task of law enforcement. In fact, he purchased a half interest in the Lone Star Dance Hall and Saloon to ensure his place at the gaming tables with his somewhat rowdy cronies.

His game leg did keep him from anything more active than patrolling the streets. It was jocularly rumored that, in making his rounds, Bat intimidated would-be offenders with the dazzling elegance of his attire—"gold-mounted spurs, a crimson Mexican sash, a red silk neckerchief and gray sombrero with a rattlesnake band, silver-plated and ivory-handled revolvers, silver-studded belt and holsters." The ivory-handled revolvers rarely came into play. As noted, Bat Masterson's record in Dodge was relatively bloodless.

Charles E. Bassett, sheriff of Ford County at this time, and his deputy Billy Tilghman were two other noted lawmen of the West. Perhaps it is to Bassett's credit that he had no sensational reputation as gunfighter, though he generally got his man. Charlie was only twenty-six when elected to office for the first of three terms. In fact, almost all who helped to keep the peace in Dodge seemed exceptionally young for such responsibility. Perhaps men matured earlier and more quickly by being forced to cope with the hard, precarious conditions of the West.

William Matthew Tilghman was even younger than his boss, only twenty-three when deputized. He had had some scrapes with the law in his early youth, and was more than once accused of banditry (though some said it was due to a mixup of names), but he later became, according to one observer, "perhaps the greatest professional peace officer the Old West ever knew. He was modest, compassionate, but firm, and—once he had overcome his early wayward tendencies—he never deviated from the straight path of his calling."

He had chosen that path at the age of twelve when he met Wild Bill Hickok while the latter was tracking down an outlaw on the Plains near Atchison. He might have selected a better model than the controversial Hickok. But his wife, Zoe A. Tilghman, recalling what her husband had told her, wrote: "Wild Bill became the hero and pattern for adventure for young Billy. . . . For weeks he talked of Wild Bill, even dreamed of him."

> He had a pair of cap-and-ball pistols, and all the money he could get hold of he spent for caps, powder, and lead. He practiced shooting pop-shots from the hip, with both hands, in emulation of Wild Bill. Lefthand shooting was extremely hard at first; and the quick draw, and shooting as soon as the

gun was leveled, aiming, in fact, in the very motion
of drawing it, by judgment rather than actual sight-
ing, was a refinement of skill that sometimes seemed
almost impossible. But he kept determinedly at it,
and the practice of a thousand shots told. The
time came when he could hit a rabbit or a prairie
chicken sitting in the grass thirty feet away, with a
quick pop-shot.

There were a number of others, some of them
colorful frontier characters described as "equally
comfortable on either side of the line dividing law
from order." Mysterious Dave Mather was one, accused in 1879 of conspiring with the notorious horse
thief Dutch Henry Born, but later acting as marshal
of Dodge City; ex-buffalo hunter Prairie Dog Dave
Morrow, who, even while serving as peace officer,
was something of a rake and drunk; and even John
"Doc" Holliday, the gunfighting dentist who, though
he was briefly deputized by Wyatt Earp and sometimes aided the marshal in emergencies, was more
often on the wrong side of the law than on the right.

Bat Masterson and his brothers Jim and Ed, Wyatt
Earp and brothers Morgan and Virgil, and part-
Cherokee Neal Brown, along with Charlie Bassett
and Bill Tilghman, comprised the hard core of
Dodge's police force during the boom years of the
Texas cattle drives. The town boasted that "this
coterie of peace officers could maintain law and
order in any community on earth." And among

earth's communities Dodge City was perhaps the toughest to control.

During the season of 1877 some two hundred thousand Longhorns came to the city for shipment east, and with them came the proverbial hordes of cowboys ready to throw off all restraint and turn the town into an uproar. The following spring forecast an even bigger season for the cattlemen and drovers, and for Dodge's reputation as a wild and lawless cowtown. It opened inauspiciously with the first deliberate killing of a lawman in the history of Dodge.

That April of 1878 Wyatt Earp was pursuing Dave Rudabaugh's gang of horse thieves over half the state of Kansas. Ed Masterson was serving as marshal in Wyatt's absence, supported by brother Bat as county sheriff. In spite of the one-year difference in their ages Bat always felt protective toward his older brother. He considered Ed too charitable toward his enemies, too reluctant to draw his guns and shoot to kill. Unfortunately he was right. The vanguard of cowboys arriving in Dodge that spring were quick to get out of hand. Early in March the *Globe* complained: "Some of the boys, in direct violation of the city ordinances, carry firearms on our streets without being called to account for same. They do so in such an open manner that it doesn't seem possible that our city officers are in ignorance of the fact."

Ed Masterson was well aware of this defiance of the law. In attempting to disarm a belligerent cowboy named Bob Shaw in Bat Masterson's Lone Star Saloon, a scuffle ensued in which Shaw shot the marshal in the arm. Ed, in turn, crippled the cowboy with a bullet in his thigh. When Ed recovered he found the Texans still in virtual possession of the town and eager to avenge their wounded comrade. Two in particular, Jack Wagner and Alf Walker, challenged the marshal's authority when he intervened in a fracas at the Lady Gay and ordered them to drop their guns.

Seeming at first to comply, Walker and Wagner surrendered their revolvers and waited till Ed had left the building. Then they followed him out and, with a gun that he had kept concealed, Wagner fired point-blank at the marshal's back. Mortally wounded, his clothes aflame from the close-range blast, Ed managed to reach the door of George Hoover's Alamo Saloon, where he quietly said, "I'm shot, George," and collapsed. Forty minutes later he was dead.

Bat Masterson, rounding a corner of Front Street, witnessed the shooting from sixty feet away. Wagner saw Bat first, and took no chances. He started firing recklessly. Bat ignored the bullets, drew his silver-plated six-guns, and, taking careful aim, fired two shots from each. The first struck Walker in the stomach, fatally wounding him. The next three plowed into Wagner, one piercing his lung, two shattering his arm. Wagner staggered into the Lone Star, gasping to saloon man Ham Bell:

"Catch me! I'm dying!"

The normally sympathetic Bell was unmoved. "This is as good a place to die as any," he replied, and let him fall.

When Bat Masterson reached Hoover's saloon and found Ed dying, it was the first time anyone had seen the sheriff weep. "This will go hard with Ma," he said. The city shared his grief. The next day Dodge was decked with crepe, all business was suspended, and the city bowed its collective heads respectfully as the funeral cortege proceeded to Fort Dodge, where Ed was buried in the military cemetery.

More than anything else, Ed Masterson's death awoke Dodge City to its peril from the constantly invading Texans. Much as the money they brought contributed to the town's prosperity, the cost was too high to be overlooked for long. Once again Mayor Kelley sent for Wyatt Earp, urging him to hasten his return. In the next few months of 1878 a new and significant chapter would be written in Dodge City's history.

6

Cowboys and Indians

I saw the Injuns coming, I heard them give a yell,
  My feelings at that moment no human tongue can
    tell;
I saw their glittering lances and their arrows round
    me flew,
  And all my strength it left me and all my cour-
    age, too.

Our Singing Country

For many years the Santa Fe Trail continued to be
a factor in the life of Dodge. Though the completion
of the railroad tended to reduce the traffic somewhat,
heavily laden wagon trains still made the long trek
across Kansas from Missouri to New Mexico—a constant provocation to the warlike Indians of the Plains.
As Bob Wright recorded:

  I have seen with my glass, from the top of my
  building at the ranch, two or three hundred wagons
  and two thousand head of mules and oxen, all wait-

ing for the river to go down so that they could cross. And I have watched a band of Indians charge upon them like an avalanche, kill the poor, panic-stricken drivers as easily and unmercifully as a bunch of hungry wolves would destroy a flock of sheep. Then the savages would jump off their horses long enough to tear the reeking scalps from their victims' heads and dash off after fresh prey.

The plumed and painted warrior of the Plains, superbly mounted on his Arabian-descended steed, is the popular stereotype of the North American Indian. Actually, he was unique among his race. And the distinction lay with the Indian pony, descended from horses left behind by the early Spaniards and since tamed and trained to perfection by the Indians.

The mustang made the Indians not only proud and independent; it made them mobile and expert hunters as well as formidable fighters. Unlike the Eastern tribes, they were strictly nomads, following the herds from range to range, from season to season —for the buffalo was basic to their life. While the white hunter at first sought only the hides for profit, leaving the carcasses to rot, the Plains Indians used everything from nose to tail. Those who slaughtered the animals for sport or greed were unforgivable and hated enemies.

It was these considerations that made the Indians of the Plains the greatest single obstacle to American expansion in the West. The tribes of the East had offered no such savage opposition; they had been driven across the Mississippi to reservations in the present area of Oklahoma. But throughout the early years of Dodge the prairie Indians—Cheyennes, Comanches, Arapahoes, Kiowas, and Apaches—were lords of the range—especially the fierce Cheyennes, known among their brothers as the Beautiful People of the Plains.

The United States Cavalry, glamorized in the sagas of the West, was at first outfought and outmaneuvered. A young officer from Fort Dodge asserted that "our mounted men, though armed with revolvers, were in general not a match for the mounted Indians with their bows and arrows." A Cheyenne or Comanche, controlling his horse with knees alone and thus keeping both hands free—one to hold the arrows and the other to release his bow—could shoot under the neck or belly of his horse's body.

The early settlers of southern Kansas and of Dodge lived in constant danger from the prairie tribes. Before 1870 some 225,000 Indians roamed the Plains, as intent on driving out the hunter as the hunter was in slaughtering the buffalo. There was no serious effort toward peaceful coexistence. A few frontiersmen like Charlie Rath, who spoke both Arapaho and Cheyenne, made a fortune trading with the Indians and cheating them outrageously (cheating, in Charlie's eyes, was simply "Yankee shrewdness"). The somewhat self-righteous Bob Wright, later a leading citizen of Dodge, freely sold whiskey to the Indians in defiance of government regulations; while local cattlemen operated "whiskey ranches" on the prairies around Dodge, partly for profit, partly to keep the Indians appeased or stupefied.

But in general, Dodge City agreed, there was no living amicably with the Indians. "'Tain't no use shakin' hands and talkin' peace with 'em," said one old timer. "Might makes right with 'em every time." And so no truce, no quarter, was given, in the slightest chance encounter. The wagonmaster on the trail, the man riding shotgun on the stage, and above all the buffalo hunter put their lives at stake each time they crossed the Plains.

Survival depended on an understanding not of the red man's ways alone but of prairie lore as well. Kit Carson, whose legend hangs like a banner over Dodge, knew both. When Kit was guiding five hunters on muleback over the Plains they passed a herd of buffalo trotting downwind—sure sign that Indians were close. Seconds later the Comanches showed themselves on the horizon, two hundred painted warriors, mounted on their high-strung and perceptive ponies. What chance had Carson's little party, outnumbered thirty to one, with no ridge or rock to hide behind, and with only a limited supply of bullets for their muzzle-loading rifles?

Barking an order, Kit leaped from his mule, slashed the animal's throat, and dropped behind the carcass. The other five followed suit, making a circle of the slaughtered mules. When the charging Indians were all but on top of them, lances raised and leveled for the kill, what happened? The ponies suddenly screamed and reared, spoiling their riders' aim and swerving past the huddled group to leave the spent lances quivering in barren soil.

The Indians circled back and charged again, this time with hands locked on their bows and arrows. Again the ponies balked and swerved and the arrows sprayed harmlessly overhead while the Indian braves were carried well beyond their target. Carson had learned one lesson well: that an Indian pony shied at the smell of blood and would not come near a slaughtered mule.

The Comanches tried a different strategy. On their next and last assault they sent their medicine man ahead, waving his rattle to dispel whatever charm protected the white hunter. This time Kit's party did not hold their fire. Six bullets swept the medicine man from his horse like a bolt from heaven— a sure sign to the Comanches that the gods had turned against them. The siege was lifted; Kit's band trudged wearily but gratefully over the long miles back to Dodge.

More than one Dodgeite tangled with the Indians on the Plains. As a buffalo hunter Bat Masterson was surrounded by five braves of Bear Shield's tribe. While one kept Masterson covered with his lance, the others stripped him of his rifle and revolver, then, for good measure, bashed his skull with the rifle barrel. Wobbly and dripping blood, Bat staggered back to camp, where his companions advised him to forget the incident. There were probably more Indians around and they had better clear out as soon as it was dark.

But Bat couldn't forget it, any more than he could have forgotten the pay that had been due him from the crooked foreman of the Santa Fe. That night, while the rest of the party returned to Dodge, he scouted the prairies till he uncovered Bear Shield's camp, with its herd of Indian ponies. It took only a few surreptitious moments; then he was heading back to Dodge with as fine a bunch of stolen horseflesh as the town had seen. The forty ponies brought twelve hundred dollars on the local market, and Bat's injured pride was recompensed.

Theoretically, by a treaty signed in 1876, the Plains tribes were confined to Indian Territory, with the right to hunt south of the Arkansas River "so long as the buffalo may range thereon in such numbers as to justify the chase." But how long before the while man would destroy the herds? Of 3,700,000 buffalo killed between 1872 and 1874, only 150,000 were slain by Indians, and then only for essential food.

The arrival of the cattle drives after 1874 only added to the Indians' aggravation. Herders were not only forced to pay a toll on passing through Indian Territory, in cattle or in cash; but once across the Arkansas River they were prey to more vicious, hostile measures. The Indians hated the cowboys as much the hunters since their cattle depleted the grass the buffalo lived on. One infuriated chief appealed to the fort's commander for a cannon. The colonel was outraged.

"You mean you want to shoot my men with cannon!"

"No," the chief reassured him. "Kill soldiers with clubs, shoot cowboys with cannon."

General Philip Sheridan's classic statement, "The only good Indian is a dead Indian," expressed the military's attitude toward the tribes. And the way to kill off the Indian was to kill off the buffalo on which his livelihood depended. The strife that followed, the so-called Buffalo War, was a last desperate attempt by the Indians to save the animal from extinction. Their own lands were supposedly protected. But as the herds in the north diminished, the white hunters began edging south. Led by Joshua Mooar, a group of Dodge City hunters approached Major Richard Dodge, commander of the fort, and asked what he would do if they hunted on the forbidden Indian ranges south of the Arkansas. The major replied with arch evasiveness, "Well, boys, if I were hunting buffalo I'd go where the buffalo are."

Dodge City took the major at his word. In the early spring of 1874 Charlie Rath called a meeting of buffalo hunters camped in Dodge. He proposed that they invade the Indian preserve and establish a fortified outpost there. There were, in fact, the ruins of an old Mexican fort on the banks of the Canadian River that would serve the purpose. All it needed was a little fixing up.

The plan met with immediate approval. Assured that Rath & Wright's firm would keep them supplied with food and ammunition, and also buy the hides they garnered, a sizable expedition set out for the ruins of the fort. Among the group was the twenty-year-old Bat Masterson and his young companions Billy Dixon, Brick Bond, and Billy Ogg. Also with the expedition were blacksmith Tom O'Keefe, saloonkeeper Jim Hanrahan, the merchant Fred Leonard, and William Olds and his wife Sybil, who proposed to run a restaurant at the camp.

The adobe foundations of the fort were topped with thick sod walls and roofs, housing Leonard's and Rath's stores, a blacksmith shop, and Hanrahan's saloon. A start was made at erecting a stockade around the settlement, now christened Adobe Walls. But it was never finished. When not absorbed with drinking and gambling, the hunters were occupied with target practice. It was late in June and any moment now the buffalo would be coming.

More than the buffalo were coming. Word of this invasion of their sacred hunting grounds spread swiftly through the neighboring tribes. Chief Santanta of the Kiowas, most dreaded of Plains warriors, rallied seven hundred Kiowas, Comanches, and Cheyennes, and led them on a campaign to destroy Adobe Walls. They were assured of easy victory by their infallible medicine man, Isatai, whose magic was such that he could "vomit wagonloads of ammunition from his belly and arrest a white man's bullet in mid-flight."

There are many strange and contradictory reports on the subsequent Battle of Adobe Walls. One account claims that Charlie Rath and other sponsors of the expedition learned from Indian informers of the threatened attack, but withheld this information lest the hunters be dissuaded from their purpose of acquiring hides. It is true that Isatai was a friend of Charlie Rath; true, also, that other merchants hastily returned to Dodge to "attend to local business."

In any event, there were only twenty-seven men (and one lone woman) at Adobe Walls when the dreaded cry of "Indians!" went up at dawn, June 28. Brick Bond never heard the warning. He had started off earlier with a load of hides, headed for

Dodge, in spite of the obvious danger to anyone traveling alone through Indian Territory.

Of four men outside the stockade who were first to catch sight of the mounted hordes on the horizon, three were killed and scalped in the initial, stunning charge. Only Billy Ogg, who had gone to the corral to check the horses, barely made it to Hanrahan's saloon. Fortunately, a number of restless hunters had been drinking through the night in the saloon and, with the frontiersman's capacity to handle liquor, were well awake and quick to barricade the doors and windows. Fortunately too the walls and roofs, being made of sod, failed to catch fire when the attackers flung their flaming arrows at the buildings.

It was no doubt an awe-inspiring spectacle as wave after wave of mounted warriors—in rainbow-colored war paint, brightly feathered headdresses, lances gleaming in the dawn—swept down upon the adobe shelters, rearing their ponies to try to batter down the doors, hurling their lances and firing through the windows. In fact, outlying tribes with no practical interest in the engagement rode from miles around to witness the expected slaughter, like the audience at a Roman circus.

Of the twenty-seven defenders, only fourteen were hunters and marksmen. The rest were blacksmiths, bartenders, cooks, and freighters, although all pitched in to man the ports and windows. The little group,

"Windwagons," such as the above, were tried on the plains as a replacement for the horse-drawn "prairie schooner." *Frank Leslie's Illustrated Newspaper*

Wild Bill Hickok, as marshal of Wichita, set a dubious precedent for cow-town lawmen. *The Kansas State Historical Society, Topeka*

William F. "Buffalo Bill" Cody, prairie scout and crack-shot hunter, became the star of a touring Wild West Show. *The Kansas State Historical Society, Topeka*

The first house on the site of Dodge City, built of sod by H. L. Sitler in 1871. *The Kansas State Historical Society, Topeka*

George M. Hoover, wholesale liquor dealer and onetime mayor of Dodge, opened the first tent saloon in "Buffalo City." *The Kansas State Historical Society, Topeka*

Robert M. Wright, pioneer merchant and one of the founders of Dodge City. *The Kansas State Historical Society, Topeka*

An early photo of Front Street, September 1872. The Wright Supply House is in the left foreground; the Santa Fe Depot and tracks are on the right. *The Kansas State Historical Society, Topeka*

Some forty thousand buffalo hides are piled by the Santa Fe tracks at Dodge in 1874, awaiting shipment to the Eastern markets. *The Kansas State Historical Society, Topeka*

Buffalo bones piled beside the railroad track, awaiting shipment to Eastern markets, marked the end of the great herds that once roamed the Plains around Dodge City. *Fort Dodge Historical Society*

An early locomotive of the Atchison, Topeka & Santa Fe Railroad arrives at Dodge City in the fall of 1872. *The Kansas City Historical Society, Topeka*

Wright, Beverley & Company, in this two-story brick building on Front Street, was the city's leading mercantile establishment. *The Kansas State Historical Society, Topeka*

As the gun-topped pole suggests, Fred C. Zimmermann's store was
a leading provider of two essential Dodge commodities: firearms
and ammunition. *The Kansas State Historical Society, Topeka*

J. Mueller's "Sign of the Big Boot" was a familiar Front Street land-
mark in the 1870's. *Fort Dodge Historical Society*

H. B. ("Ham") Bell, ranchman, sheriff, and proprietor of the Elephant Barn
Livery Stable. *The Kansas State Historical Society, Topeka*

This view of North Front Street in 1875 shows Rath & Wright's General Store on the far left, the Long Branch Saloon, and George M. Hoover's wholesale liquor store. *Fort Dodge Historical Society*

The north side of Front Street in the late 1870's. The sign atop the advertising placard reads: "The Carrying of Fire Arms Strictly Prohibited." *The Kansas State Historical Society, Topeka*

South of the tracks, below the "dead line," Dodge City lacked the more solid, respectable look of Front Street's North Side. *W. S. Campbell Collection, Western History Collections, University of Oklahoma Library*

Billy Brooks was an early marshal of Dodge City, but was hanged as a horse thief ten years later. *Fort Dodge Historical Society*

James "Dog" Kelley, the popular sportsman and saloon proprietor, served three terms as mayor of Dodge City. *The Kansas State Historical Society, Topeka*

Stampedes were the major peril on the cattle drives from Texas to Dodge City.

Longhorn cattle were frequently driven through the streets of Dodge to the Santa Fe Railroad shipping pens. *The Kansas State Historical Society, Topeka*

"Hurrahing" the town was a popular pastime when the cattle-herding cowboys arrived from Texas. *Frank Leslie's Illustrated Newspaper*

too, was scattered among four buildings. Bat Masterson and Billy Dixon commanded Hanrahan's saloon, O'Keefe rallied those in the blacksmith shop, Fred Leonard and Andy Johnson directed the defense of Leonard and Rath's stores.

Hour after hour the Indians charged upon the camp, intent on exhausting the defenders' ammunition. Their fighting spirit seemed to be inspired by a bugler trumpeting United States Army signals, who the defenders guessed to be a deserter from the Union Army. When Hanrahan's saloon ran out of bullets, volunteers raced across the intervening space to get a fresh supply from Rath's and Leonard's stores. There was no lack of ammunition in the camp itself; the hunters had come well prepared for buffalo.

But they had counted on the river for their water. Now, as the sun beat down on the adobe roofs, their thirst developed into torture. Young Andy Johnson, who manned one of the windows at Rath's store (so scared, he admitted, he hardly knew what he was shooting at), left his post to start digging in the gravel floor. Six feet down he struck water, and passed it out—a godsend for the exhausted hunters.

Stung by this resistance, the Indians stepped up the fury of their attacks. They tried everything—climbing up on the roofs to hack out holes through which to shoot, compressing their horses three abreast to be hurled like battering rams against the doors. But the mud huts held, and the buffalo guns began to take their toll. How many Indians fell that first day? Nobody kept count. But when the braves withdrew at sundown they left fifteen of their own dead on the field, along with the three Americans. The corral was strewn with the corpses of twenty-eight oxen and fifty-six horses—almost all the draft animals accompanying the expedition.

The nighttime lull in the fighting allowed the defenders time to bury the dead. Fifteen stakes in the stockade wall were sharpened, and a severed Indian head was impaled on each, facing outward, eyes propped open, to greet the enemy when he returned. This grisly task was barely finished and the hunters back inside their walls when a familiar voice shouted to be admitted. It was Brick Bond. His wagon had bogged down in treacherous sand and he had ridden one of the horses back to camp, astonished to see the row of staring heads.

How had he passed through the Indian lines unharmed? Nobody had an answer. Years later Brick asked Chief Little Robe of the Cheyennes: "You must have seen me; why did you let me get through alive?" The answer: Brick had never been seen bearing arms against the Cheyennes, so "Indian no want to kill a friend."

The following day was a repetition of the first: swift charges, a shower of arrows, then a quick retreat while the next wave of Indians hit the fort. Perhaps the young marksman Billy Dixon had learned a bit of Kit Carson's strategy. Among the distant Indians he identified their medicine man, Isatai (who had been flogged by his comrades for failing to stop the white man's bullets, but was being given a second chance). Now, with Brick Bond as a witness, Dixon brought Isatai within the sights of his Sharps fifty and drilled him through from a distance of about a mile—the longest shot in the history of the Southwest Plains.

Billy's marksmanship made the braves more wary. They began to keep their distance from the long-range buffalo guns. As a result, white hunters caught on the prairies when the shooting started began slipping back into Adobe Walls. Six of their number, they reported, had been trapped and slain. As more arrived, the diminishing food supply presented a new crisis. A trader named Jim Langton, worried perhaps about the thousands of buffalo hides he'd stacked outside the stockade, offered two hundred dollars to anyone who would ride to Dodge for help. Henry Lease, one of the hunters, volunteered, taking the horse which Brick Bond had returned with. Before sneaking out that night, Lease solemnly shook hands with all his comrades; nobody, himself included, expected him to return alive.

Under cover of darkness, however, Lease got through. He reported to Charlie Rath the dire predicament of the hunters, then raced to Fort Dodge

to alert the United States Cavalry. But there would
be no cavalry riding, in theatrical tradition, to the
rescue. Major Richard Dodge, partly responsible for
the crisis with his advice to "go where the buffalo
are," had been replaced by Major Charles E. Compton. Compton was outraged by the hunters' invasion
of Indian Territory. So was Governor Thomas A. Os-
born of Kansas, who, when appealed to, refused
"to send troops to protect an unlawful trading post."

That left only Charlie Rath and Bob Wright to
take action and, pricked by their consciences perhaps, they organized a relief force of fifty-nine armed
volunteers and a train of oxen-drawn wagons, led
by the buffalo hunter and scout, Tom Nixon. On
June 30 the expedition headed bravely for Adobe
Walls.

Back at Adobe Walls the situation was becoming
desperate. The defenders had no realistic hope
that Henry Lease had gotten through to Dodge. Some
seventy Indians had been killed, by estimate, but it
scarcely made a dent in their surrounding ranks.
The hunters held on through a third day of assaults and then a fourth day. On the morning of
the fifth day William Olds mounted to the roof
and sounded the familiar alarm, "They're comin'!"
As he hastily climbed down, his musket caught on
a rung of the ladder and blew his head off. He
died in the arms of his wife, the only woman in

the camp and one whose nerves and resolution never cracked.

On the sixth day things seemed hopeless. The little garrison, now numbering thirty-five, decided to chance it and fight their way back to Dodge. That night, Billy Dixon, a former scout for the United States Army, led them by little-known paths toward the Kansas border. Halfway to their destination they met Rath's relief train. The nightmare ended; they returned to Dodge in triumph. And their plight had not cooled the hunters' penchant for collecting trophies. Charlie Rath's wife Carrie, who rode out to greet them, was horrified at the grisly collection of Indian scalps, bullet-riddled shields, and bloodied lances.

The first week in August, some forty days after the siege of Adobe Walls began, the army finally sent a punitive expedition into the territory with Bat Masterson and Billy Dixon as civilian scouts. It was a small force; most of the troops were needed to protect the town. They found Adobe Walls deserted and reduced again to ruins. Inspired by their victory, the Indians were moving north for retaliatory raids on Dodge and other settlements along the Arkansas.

Recorded David K. Strate: "Several emboldened war parties attacked railroad trains as they labored toward Dodge City. It was not unusual for the 'iron horses' to arrive pockmarked with bullet holes and bristling with arrows. Wild-eyed passengers, most of whom had just seen their first Indians . . . cursed the railroad for exposing paying customers to the hazards of Plains warfare. The railroad in turn petitioned the military for armed guards to accompany each run along the route from Topeka to Dodge City."

Adobe Walls was a peak point in the Buffalo War that drenched the plains of Kansas in a bloodbath. Outlying ranchers, railroad crews, and frontier camps bore the brunt of the assaults. A group of surveyors for the Santa Fe was ambushed, and half a dozen lost their scalps. Scores of deaths were reported on the Plains, where the buffalo hunters had become the hunted. Many hunters scurried to Fort Dodge for safety, while citizens in the town clung to their homes in terror at this new wave of atrocities.

Perhaps the town's salvation did, in bitter fact, lie with the extermination of the buffalo. By 1877 the northern herds were all but gone, and the Plains tribes were reduced by sickness and starvation to a fraction of their original numbers, several hundred at the most. Against them were mobilized U.S. troops equipped with repeating rifles and artillery. One by one the Indians were forced into subjection—Santanta and Lone Wolf with their mighty Kiowas, Dull Knife and his proud Cheyennes.

They were herded back to their reservations south

of Kansas, where there were not enough buffalo left
to eat, and some survived on their butchered horses.
To Dull Knife's Cheyennes, who had come origi-
nally from the Dakotas, this was unbearable humiliation. In the unfamiliar climate and inhospitable land
they wasted and watched their squaws and children
die. In early September of 1878, Dull Knife told
his followers: "This is not our land. We go home.
If we must fight and die on the way, our names will
be cherished and remembered by our people."

In open defiance of the troops at Dodge, three
hundred Cheyennes, two thirds of them women and
children, started the long hegira north to the Black
Hills. There were not enough horses or food, but
they would get those on the way. On either side
of the widely spread column rode ninety-one braves,
"strongest of heart in a proud, doomed tribe." A
small infantry unit from Fort Dodge was sent to
intercept them; six bluecoats were killed or wounded
and the rest withdrew to remain as a tiny garrison
at the depleted fort.

At first, as the Indians crossed into Kansas, they
refrained from any wholesale plundering of ranches
in their path, stealing only what horses and food
they needed to continue on their way. But as the
ranchers and cowboys mobilized and started sniping
at the column, the Cheyennes responded in kind,
and an all-out, running war developed. In mid-
September word reached Dodge of their approach,

and Billy Tilghman and Bob Wright went out as scouts. They reported that several cattle drives on their way to Dodge had been raided and a number of drovers had been killed and mutilated.

Overnight the city became an armed camp. Mayor Kelley issued weapons to all able-bodied men, Texans and Kansans alike, who buried their differences long enough to present a united front. Kelley also telegraphed the then Governor George T. Anthony: "No U.S. troops here, and no arms at the post. The country filled with Indians. Send arms immediately." A committee of citizens also telegraphed the governor, "Indians are murdering and burning houses within three miles of town. Can you send us arms and ammunition?" That the governor hesitated might have been due to his wonder that a city which lived by the gun demanded still more guns. But he ordered that a hundred rifles and seven thousand rounds of ammunition be dispatched to Dodge (later he was going to have to sue the town to get them back).

While a Santa Fe locomotive manned by cowboys with rifles and revolvers shuttled back and forth across the town, trying to guess where the fleeing tribe might try to ford the Arkansas, Wyatt Earp rounded up eighty of the city's tougher customers and led them out to intercept the Indians. They had no trouble finding the column, but the Cheyennes were too wily to be drawn into an open fight. A series of running skirmishes were all that Earp's forces could achieve. At sundown they withdrew to wait till morning to renew the attack. But at dawn the Indians had disappeared.

They had left the vicinity of Dodge with ten white men dead, and 640 cattle and horses stolen or destroyed. Yet the war-weary, tattered Indians were going to their doom. Two strong cavalry units were converging on the column from both sides, avoiding a direct encounter but picking off the warriors one by one, then turning their rifles on the sick, the old, the very young who lagged behind. This war of attrition followed the Cheyennes to within a few miles of their destination until, faint from wounds, hunger, and exhaustion, they were surrounded and taken prisoner.

The noble band of ninety-one Cheyenne braves had been reduced to a pitiful seven. These were delivered to Fort Leavenworth, where Bat Masterson and Charlie Bassett, absent in Kansas City when the fighting started, were sent to bring them back to Dodge for trial. The cars of the Santa Fe that carried the prisoners from Leavenworth to Dodge were regarded as a traveling menagerie. Crowds assembled at the wayside stations to gape at the "murderous savages." The same circus atmosphere prevailed when the Indians reached Dodge. Gawking citizens insisted that the braves be paraded on the streets, and photographed beside their conquerors. Thus humiliated, one chieftain tried to kill himself with a stolen knife.

An Eastern-trained lawyer appointed to defend the Cheyennes from charges of murder declared that they could never receive a fair trial in Dodge or any other Kansas town where hatred of the Indian was so apparent. He was wrong. With an American penchant for the underdog, voices were raised in sympathy for the humiliated braves. Outspoken editor Nicholas Klaine of the Dodge City *Times* declared in effect that they deserved death before dishonor; that speedy execution was better than the cruelty of the treatment they received. The jury, regarding these pitiful remnants of a once-proud tribe, pronounced them "not guilty for lack of evidence."

So ended the last great stand of the Cheyennes, not with a bang but a whimper. Dodge never again had cause to give much thought to Indians. They were well gone, like the buffalo; cattle was the big thing now—and while the Indians might steal a few head now and then, and even a few horses, they had ceased to be a menace. Even Fort Dodge was declared no longer necessary, and four years later was abandoned and its garrison distributed to other posts.

Yet, like the tame buffalo who roamed the streets of Dodge as pets and sentimental symbols of the past, a few Indians remained as second-class citizens of the community. They cadged drinks, did occasional menial labor, and sold buffalo robes to cattlemen and cowboys. But purchasers were warned to spread the blankets over anthills before using, to get rid of lice.

7

Two-gun Metropolis

Some there was that claimed they saw it, as the
    killer tried to draw;
  But there's no one knows for certain just exactly
    what they saw.
I'll agree the shootin' started quick as Blake had
    made his start—
  Then a brace of bullets hit him fair and certain
    through the heart.

                                        The Killer

The story is told of the young Dodge mother left
alone with her baby while the father was hunting
on the Plains. A sinister-looking tramp approached
the lonely shack. She grabbed her husband's six-
gun from its holster hanging on the wall. Her heart
and hand trembled as she tried to hold the revolver
steady, pointed at the door. Then she remembered
her husband's warning: Don't try to outshoot a man
who's more experienced with guns than you are.

She dropped the revolver in the baby's crib and prepared to defy or conciliate the stranger as he forced his way into the cabin. The tramp made his entrance and, finding her alone, swaggered across the room with a suggestive leer. Then he glanced into the crib. His expression changed. Recoiling, he sped out the door and fled. With overwhelming relief the woman rushed to her infant in the crib. He was teething and, revolver in mouth, was chewing on the barrel. Even the hardiest desperado might well take flight at the sight of a scarcely weaned baby with a six-gun in his teeth.

Apocryphal or not, the tale illustrates a truth. Almost from infancy the gun was as much a part of the frontier male as his hands and arms. Notable gunmen such as Billy the Kid, Doc Holliday, and Wild Bill Hickok had fired to kill while still in their early teens. While the average youngster may have learned to shoot for purposes of hunting and protection, he soon discovered that the gun and how he used it defined his position in society, and assured equality among his fellow men.

The Sharps fifty buffalo rifle was the early weapon on the Plains. Along with the twelve-gauge shotgun it remained a part of almost every hunter's arsenal. But long before the 1870s came the Colt revolver, in which a rotating cylinder holding a bullet in each of six chambers fired through a single barrel. It was really six guns in one, and hence generally

referred to as the "six-gun" or "six-shooter." It replaced the single-shot pistol that took time to re-
load between each shot: if, with a pistol, the first
bullet missed its mark, the gunman might never
have another chance.

Invented in the 1830s by young Samuel Colt,
who whittled his first model out of wood, the revolver helped establish the Republic of Texas in
the hands of Texas Rangers. After numerous im-
provements and refinements it evolved into the Colt
forty-five-caliber Peacemaker, which became the
favorite weapon of marshals, sheriffs, and gunslinging outlaws. Lawmen Bat Masterson and Wyatt
Earp, as well as gunfighters Clay Allison and Ben
Thompson, staked their lives on the forty-five.

As one historian of the Plains expressed it, "If
the horse elevated man and enlarged his sphere
of influence, as it apparently did, the six-shooter
increased his power in every situation in which he
found himself. The Plainsman liked to say, and it
became his saying, that God made some men large
and some men small, but Colonel Colt made all men
equal." In fact, the term "equalizer," sometimes
still appearing in the chronicles of the West, origi-
nated in the Kansas cowtowns.

Tolerance, and even respect, for the use of guns
was deeply embedded in frontier justice. A cowboy
who had participated in a gunfight on the Plaza

was brought before Judge V. B. Osborne as a matter of routine.

"How do you plead?" the justice asked him—again a matter of routine.

"Guilty, your honor," the innocent Texan replied.

The judge was outraged. The fight had been fairly conducted, face to face, with both men equally prepared.

"Young man," shouted Osborne, "don't ever plead guilty in this court again or I'll throw you into jail!"

Some gun-toters had their weapons custom made. Bat Masterson ordered his Colt forty-fives built according to his own design, nickel-plated, with special sights and gutta-percha handles, and, he demanded, "easy on the trigger." In fact the Colt revolvers, along with other weapons used in Kansas cowtowns, were subjected to alterations and adjustments by the user. The catch that held and freed the hammer was often filed down to quicken the release and give "hair-trigger" action. Sometimes the trigger was dispensed with altogether, either removed or fastened back against the guard, in which case the gun was fired by thumbing or stroking the hammer.

Modern Western motion pictures often show a gunman "fanning" his revolver as he fires at an opponent. With the right hand holding the gun, the left hand sweeps back and forth over the hammer, cocking and releasing it with every stroke, as fast as the gunman can move his forearm. Wyatt Earp, who admittedly was an expert, had little use for this spectacular but tricky method. "A skillful gun-fanner," he observed, "could fire five shots from a forty-five so rapidly that the individual reports were indistinguishable, but what could happen to him in a gunfight was pretty close to murder."

Wyatt mentions the custom of keeping five bullets in a gun equipped to fire six. Among the favorite comedy acts at the Comique Theater or the Lady Gay were those depicting a clumsy sheriff or Eastern greenhorn aiming at an enemy and shooting off his own big toe or inflicting some equally ridiculous injury. Something like this occurred to Wyatt Earp himself. During his first term as marshal in Dodge, the local press reported:

> Last Sunday night, while policeman Earp was sitting with three others in the back room of a saloon, his revolver slipped from its holster. In falling to the floor, the hammer, which was resting on the cap, is supposed to have struck the chair, causing a discharge of one of the chambers. The ball passed through his coat, struck the wall, then glanced off and passed out through the ceiling. It was a narrow escape and caused a lively stampede from the room. One of the demoralized patrons was under the impression that someone had fired through the window from outside.

Some years later, Wyatt elaborated on the incident:

> I have often been asked why five shots without reloading were all a top notch gun-fighter ever fired, when his guns were chambered for six cartridges. The answer is, merely, safety. To ensure against accidental discharge of the gun . . . due to hair-trigger adjustment, the hammer always rested on an empty chamber.

In fact, the marshal explained further, the number of cartridges a man carried in his six-gun was an indication of his rank among gunfighters of that era. Only an amateur or show-off would carry a gun with all six chambers loaded. After his own near-suicide in the saloon, the first chamber of Wyatt's six-gun always remained empty.

Not only the professional gunfighters but the Texas cowboys as well—in fact virtually every man in Dodge—carried two guns, one on either hip. These were positioned according to the length of his reach, the butts touching the palms of his hands when his arms were at his side. A few gunmen wore their holsters slightly above the hips, crossing their arms when they reached for their revolvers.

Along with the glamorized but treacherous method of fanning a gun was the mythical practice of "shooting from the hip," with both barrels blazing simultaneously. This rarely happened, if at all. A second gun was carried simply as a reserve, to be brought into action only when the first was emptied. Sometimes both guns might be drawn at once, since the veteran gunman was generally equally skillful with both hands; but they were rarely fired simultaneously. Even the best of gunmen could not concentrate on aiming and firing both at once with any degree of accuracy.

Yet another trick, known as the "road agent's spin," was allegedly practiced by gunman John Wesley Hardin (and has been practiced since by every youngster who has fantasized with toy guns). His victim, the first time around, was none other than Wild Bill Hickok, who ordered young Wesley to surrender his revolvers. Hardin presented them butt first, keeping his index fingers in the trigger guards; then twirled the guns up and around in a quick half circle, using his fingers as pivots, till the butts were firmly pressed against his palms and the barrels pointed at his adversary.

According to Hardin himself, Wild Bill was so intimidated that he knuckled under, and offered to treat the gunman to a drink. Which makes Hardin a likely liar. If anyone as shrewd as Hickok could not have anticipated the familiar trick, and shot Hardin through the stomach before his guns reached leveling position, then all documented stories of Wild Bill as the King of Pistoleers are false.

Swiftness and accuracy were, of course, the secret

of survival with the six-gun. Top-notch gunmen practiced for hours developing their speed and aim. A fraction of a second in the quickness of the draw could make the difference between life and death, as could a fraction of an inch in aim. At a distance of sixty feet Wild Bill Hickok, perhaps the greatest marksman in the history of the West, allegedly could split a bullet against the edge of a dime, or drive a cork through the neck of a bottle without nicking the rim.

Trick shooting such as this, along with fanning or shooting from the hip, was generally regarded with contempt by veteran marksmen. Of Wild Bill Hickok, Wyatt Earp observed, "He knew all the fancy tricks and was as good as the best at that sort of gunplay. But when he had serious business in hand, a man to get, the acid test of marksmanship, I doubt if he employed them. . . . I never saw him fan a gun, shoot from the hip, or try to fire two guns simultaneously."

The procedure of the experts was to hold the revolver, with elbow bent, six inches from the body just above the center of the waist. And "take your time" was the advice of the professionals. Time, in this case, however, meant a fraction of a second to be certain of the aim, a difference too slight for the human eye to notice. A gunfighter who was already covered by the raised and aimed revolver of an opponent might still whip out his revolver and fire before the other had time to pull the trigger. That, on the frontier, was what was meant by speed. Or, as one veteran gunman defined it: "Mentally deliberate, but muscularly faster than thought."

Another myth to be exploded, often repeated in fictional accounts of frontier life, is that of the "notched" gun—the notches on the butt of the revolver representing "credits" for the number of men the owner had dispatched. If such embellishments existed they applied to the small-time gunman anxious to build up and display his reputation—in which case the number of notches might be real or might be faked. (The experts believed that such notches would destroy the balance of the gun.) It was rumored of Bat Masterson that his favorite six-gun "carried twenty-two notches in the butt."

Fortunately, Bat had a sense of humor, and years later turned the rumor to profitable account. He was then in New York, and a rapacious gun collector called at his office, pleading with Bat to sell him, at any price, the gun with the twenty-two notches. Of course there was no such article. But, to get rid of the pest who promised to persist in his offer, Bat went to a nearby pawnship, bought an ancient Colt revolver, and with his penknife cut twenty-two notches in the butt. When the collector was finally offered the relic at his own inflated price, he was overwhelmed by his good fortune. He asked if it

was true that every notch meant a man killed by
the weapon.

"I didn't tell him yes, and I didn't tell him no,"
Bat afterward related, "and I didn't exactly lie to
him. I simply said I hadn't counted either Mexicans
or Indians, and he went away tickled to death."

An interesting change in the Colt forty-five Peacemaker was projected by a writer of Wild West
fiction born under the multiple name of Edward
Zane Carroll Judson, but using the pseudonym Ned
Buntline. From a life of picaresque adventure, much
of it at sea, he had chosen the pen name Buntline
from the rope controlling the bottom of a square
sail. Now he was dedicated to the drama of the
wild and wooly West, and wrote four hundred novels
on the subject. He befriended William Cody, whom
he christened "Buffalo Bill," and Wild Bill Hickok,
both of whom joined him later in staging Wild
West Shows throughout the East.

Much of Buntline's fiction material came from the
lives of Dodge City's famous men of law and their
valiant deeds with the six-gun. Partly to gain publicity for himself, and partly to show his gratitude
to his hero prototypes, Buntline had the Colt factory
produce a number of forty-five Peacemakers with
barrels a foot in length, or four inches longer than
standard. Each was accompanied by a special hand-
tooled holster designed for what he named "the
Buntline Special." These he presented to his favorite

law officers of Dodge: Wyatt Earp, Bat Masterson, Bill Tilghman, Charlie Bassett, and Neal Brown.

"There was a lot of talk in Dodge about the Specials slowing us on the draw," related Wyatt. "Bat and Bill Tilghman cut off the barrels to make them standard length, but Bassett, Brown, and I kept ours as they came. Mine was my favorite over any other gun." One thing that endeared the Buntline Special to the marshal was the longer barrel, which gave additional reach to his buffaloing of a victim—by which he simply knocked him out, using the weapon as a club.

While the six-gun as a tool of trade, whether that of the gunman or law-enforcement officer, was grimly associated with interment on Boot Hill, it also had its lighter, even festive, side. It could be an instrument of innocent amusement, hopefully no more lethal than the firecrackers that were set off on the Fourth and almost every other holiday. For, perhaps in contrast to the lonely silent prairies, the Texas cowboys loved noise. No high-spirited Texan would think of entering an unfamiliar town without blasting the skies with both of his six-guns, just to let people know he had arrived. When a dozen or more hit town at once, the spent lead showered on the streets like shrapnel.

Exasperated by this practice, one old timer asked a visiting cowboy:

"Why do you fellas always gallop into town, firin'

your pistols, shootin' out the lamps, and generally scarin' the daylights outa decent folks?"

The cowboy's answer was typical. "Is there any other way of ridin' into town?"

Astonishingly few were hurt, even accidentally, in this gunplay. But when it went too far and took the form of shooting out windows, shattering storefronts and bottles behind the bars, and firing at the heels of an Eastern greenhorn just to make him dance, the marshal might step in and buffalo a few of the more boisterous offenders, dragging them off to jail to calm down.

Informal target practice often made the city sound as if it were in the center of a battle zone. But then, aside from pitching horseshoes, what else could an idle cowboy do to pass the time away? The professional, as well, had an obligation to his calling. "Most of the frontier gun-wielders practiced daily to keep their gun hands in," recalled Bat Masterson. "I have known them to stand before mirrors, going through the motions of draw-and-shoot with empty guns for an hour at a time. Outdoors they were forever firing at tin cans, bottles, telegraph poles, or any targets that offered, and shooting matches for prestige and money stakes were daily events."

It is interesting to note, in closing, that the Texas cowboy—in spite of his exposure to, and use of, guns and his reputation for firing at everything in sight when on a spree—was a notoriously poor shot. "While he was quick to draw and fire," noted one observer, "he couldn't hit a barn door. . . . He was adequate with a rifle, but hopeless with a revolver."

This was understandable. Spending sixteen to eighteen hours on the trail, he had little time for target practice; nor could his meager wages afford the hundreds of rounds of ammunition needed for such exercise. Moreover, just as his legs were bowed and weakened by hours in the saddle, so were his hands too calloused by work with reins and lariat to provide the delicate touch required for sure marksmanship.

Not only were the men of Dodge and of the Southwest frontier dedicated to the use of guns, as an almost sacred symbol of their independence and identity, but women too were forced to adjust to the traditions of the violent Kansas cowtowns. As we shall see . . .

8

The Gentle, and Not So Gentle, Sex

Now Sally was there in cowgirl clothes,
For all those cowboys were Sally's beaus.
She knew what to do when those boys got flip,
For Sal wore a six-gun on her hip.

Texas Trail to Dodge City

The plains of southwest Kansas were referred to, especially by those who lived there, as "Man's Country"—and one commentator added, "more of a man's country than any other portion of the frontier."

Yet scores, and eventually hundreds, of girls and women came to the Kansas frontier towns like Dodge, either to be with relatives or husbands or to find some over-the-rainbow utopia that the West mysteriously promised. Some came, perhaps, to escape from a restrictive or unwanted past, or even because of a secret yearning for adventure. Whatever the reason, the greatest tribute one can pay them is that they survived. Survived in spite of devastating hardships, dangers, deprivation, loneliness.

In general the flat and treeless plains that stretched for miles around Dodge City, with their interminable winds and dust, their limitless horizons dancing with grotesque mirages, the thundering herds of buffalo and cattle, the plagues of locusts, blizzards and tornadoes, droughts and prairie fires—these were just too much for them. "There was, on the Plains, too much of the unknown," wrote one perceptive chronicler, "and too little of the things they loved." It was well summed up by the heroine of a Western novel who, on crossing the Missouri River and staring out across the Plains, remarked, "Why, there isn't even a thing to *hide behind!*"

As a result, many groups migrating West to Kansas were halted by their women at the banks of the Missouri, where the last stands of timber, the marginal hills, and murmuring streams seemed to offer comfort and security. Yet those few who were raised in that desolate environment seemed constitutionally able to accept it. Annie Albright, for one, daughter of emigrant Ohio parents, was born in a sod hut outside Dodge. She cherished "the wonderful days following a rain, when the buffalo wallows were filled with beautiful shining water," and: "You just couldn't beat a prairie fire if you wanted a real thrill!"

But for those not born on the Kansas plains,

adjustment to life in Dodge was difficult. Annie's
mother, Ohio-born Josephine Albright, often cried
herself to sleep, while a housewife identified only
as Gussie Mootz expressed her feeling for the prairie
in five lines of verse:

> No knife, no sword, no arrow,
> Has the hurt and the sting
> That creeps to the marrow
> That burns, yet chills . . .
> Loneliness, loneliness that kills.

Chalkley Beeson, proprietor of the Long Branch
and owner of the COD Ranch on the fringes of
the city, summoned his Eastern bride to Dodge in
1876. Meeting her at the depot he started leading
her to Rath's boardinghouse, where he was living.
Front Street was then "in full bloom" and, according to Josie Albright:

> Chalk kept up a running conversation to divert
> her from the noises coming from the dance halls and
> saloons. "You'll like it here when you get acquainted
> with . . ." Crack! Bang! Two shots were heard com-
> ing from one of the buildings. Mrs. Beeson flew into
> the arms of her husband, begging him to take her
> home. Chalk carried her the remaining distance to
> Mrs. Rath's house where Carrie Rath, having come
> from Ohio as a bride herself, sized things up at a
> glance and, after a cup of tea, poured oil on troubled
> waters.

In the early days of Dodge the ratio of men to
women was five to one, this among the more-or-

less permanent population. Add to the male side of the ledger the hordes of transients—gamblers, hunters, gunmen, freighters, Texas cattlemen, and cowboys—and the scarcity of women gave their presence an importance far beyond their numbers.

It is perhaps only natural that women, as something of a rarity and even mystery in Dodge, sometimes became legendary figures. So we have the "Wild Huntress of the Plains" whose husband was shot by marauding Cheyennes and who ever after rode the prairies in a lone and vengeful war against the Indians. She was an indifferent shot, apparently, but the Cheyennes fled in terror at the sight of her. One Indian brave, who caught a glimpse of the wild huntress, remembered:

> She came to us in a cloud of buffalo, with black eyes glittering like a snake's, and coarse and uncombed hair that tangled itself in the wind and streamed and twisted behind her like withering vipers. A black riding habit flowed out in the strong breeze, its train slapping like crows' wings, and a black mustang fled from her lash.

Then there was the legendary "Rose of the Cimarron" who "went through a blizzard of bullets as if those leaden messengers of death were April raindrops," in a desperate attempt to join her exiled lover. There was a basis of fact to the story of Rose, namely that on the ride in question she was smuggling ammunition to her outlaw sweetheart, who was holed up on the prairie, hoping to hold off the sheriff and his deputies, who were hot upon his trail.

There was no myth, however, about Belle (or Bella) Starr, known in Dodge City as the Outlaw Queen. Belle and her renegade paramour Tom Starr rode into Dodge one afternoon and took rooms at Mrs. Kelley's boardinghouse. The next day Tom repaired to the Long Branch, where, in record time, he lost two thousand ill-gained dollars in a faro game. On reporting this to his partner, the tempestuous Belle promptly saddled up the horses and rode with Tom to the Long Branch. Here she sauntered into the gambling parlor, covered the room with her Colt six-shooter, scooped up all the money on the tables—seven thousand dollars—then backed out, leaped on her horse, and rode away with her lover. In the Long Branch at that time were cowboys, gamblers, gunmen, and killers, but, reported one of the witnesses, "at the sight of a woman outlaw holding up the place, they were too astonished to make a move."

While the term "gun moll" was yet to be coined, there were cowtown ladies not averse to violence. Fights among women in the dance halls and saloons were not uncommon. Wyatt Earp is credited with breaking up a number of hair-pulling, eye-gouging contests between embattled Cyprians, one of whom was heralded as "the White Belt Champion of Dodge." Many were handy with guns because they had to be. Others had their favored weapons. Calamity Jane warded off admirers with a kitchen cleaver; One-eyed Kate, who drove a freighter, used a bullwhip; Big Nose Kate (there were several Kates in Dodge who had to be distinguished by descriptive nicknames) got her way by means of strategy.

As Doc Holliday's wife or girl friend (no one knew for sure), Big Nose Kate Fisher saved Doc's life when the latter was jailed in Fort Griffin for shooting a fellow poker player. Kate heard of a lynching party organized to hang Doc to the nearest tree. That night she saddled two fast horses, then set fire to the building that adjoined the calaboose. As the town's male population rallied to fight the flames, Kate raced to the jail, disarmed the guard at gunpoint, and led Doc to the waiting horses. They were halfway to Dodge before the firefighters were aware of what had happened.

Big Nose Kate was allegedly more attractive than her pseudonym suggested. But her fiery temper kept Doc under tight control, as no professional gunman could have done. "Whoever it was that first called women the weaker sex," wrote the eminent cowtown doctor Arthur Hertzler, "could not have known them as we frontier doctors did." They were not always the weaker sex, in Dodge at least.

It was strange in a way that Dodge City with its emphasis on masculinity was referred to, and referred to itself, as *Queen* of the Cowtowns. Perhaps there is a parallel in the gambler's common reference to *Lady* Luck—or better yet the way salty mariners referred to their ship as *she*. All gave the feminine gender to the things they loved, which they may have secretly feared were stronger and more durable than themselves.

For it took strong women, young or old, to survive at Dodge through the boisterous peaks of its existence. The most common profession or occupation, in the early days for sure, was that of "hostess," or dance-hall girl—at the Long Branch, the Alhambra, or the less respectable Green Front Saloon on the South Side run by Rowdy Kate Lowe, another famous female character of Dodge.

Not all of these by any means were ladies of easy virtue, though they were often forced to defend their virtue by unbecoming means. Some were simply like the Japanese geishas, providing comfort and company for a cowboy who, after weeks on the trail, was looking for liquor and girls and music in that order. They encouraged the visitors to drink, accompanying them with highballs made of cold tea, just as they steered the suckers and greenhorns to the gambling tables. It was good for business. One might not defend it as a highly moral, worthy way of life, but many later became wives of the hunters and cattlemen who had, at some time in their lives, to settle down. Jim Earp, brother of Wyatt, was happily betrothed to a lady who made her living as the hostess of a brothel.

Not all these unions were blessed with heavenly bliss. Lizzie Adams, a notorious madam, married a rancher named George Palmer and tried to adjust to normal wedded life. But, according to one report, "True love never did run smooth, and did not in this instance. Lizzie brooded over the solitude of the ranch, and shortly returned to her old life of sin, whereupon her house burned down and Palmer was accused of starting the fire." Later Palmer was brutally murdered by one of Lizzie's lovers, and, like Gussie Mootz, she briefly consoled herself by writing verse.

> Take me back home again, take me back home,
> Hopeless and helpless in sorrow I roam;
> Gone are the roses that gladdened my life,
> I must toil on in the wearisome strife.

Yet wives, sweethearts, and even dance-hall girls were a real and constructive boon to the life of the Kansas cowtowns. Someday someone may write a book—not of the contributions made by American heroines, of which there are numerous examples—but of the effect that the mere *presence* of ordinary, undistinguished women had in the making of America. Jamestown is one example, where a boatload of women saved that colony from collapse. The same phenomenon occurred in other places such as Plymouth, New Orleans, and San Francisco during the birth of these communities. One questioned not their morals or their backgrounds; their presence alone was a steadying, sanity-restoring influence—as indeed it was at Dodge.

Because many of Dodge's footloose sirens came from the South and concealed their real identity, they often adopted the name of "Dixie Lee"—Dixie and Robert E. Lee being cherished names below the Mason-Dixon line. Many succumbed in their early years to the hardships of frontier life and the ever-prevalent consumption. One Dixie Lee, upon her early demise, left a fortune totaling a hundred thousand dollars accumulated in a Dodge saloon. Lawyers searching for an heir found that her father was a rural Missouri minister. Shocked to learn of his daughter's unsavory career and end, he was little consoled by the comment of a friend, "It just goes to show, Reverend, that the wages of sin are a damned sight better than the wages of virtue."

Some of the fair sex—and regardless of looks all were "fair" to those who spent most of their lives on the prairies—made their debut or gained attention through some minor incident such as this reported in the Dodge City *Times* in March 1878:

> On Wednesday a gust of wind removed seven dollars from the stocking of Alice Chambers as she was walking down Front Street. After a six-hour search participated in by all the tramps in town,

one dollar was recovered. We did suppose the Kansas wind was of a higher order and did not stoop to such larceny.

This small human-interest item might seem of little significance except that it identified a dance-hall girl by name and made her a pariah among the "respectable" women of the town. As a result, when Alice lay dying three months later in an attic room above the Lady Gay saloon, and the new pastor of the Presbyterian church, the Reverend O. W. Wright, sat with her and prayed beside her deathbed to the end, a storm of protest arose around the minister, who had visited a fallen woman in that "palace of iniquity."

Alice had the final distinction of being the only woman to be buried on Boot Hill.

Of all the women whom Dodge remembers, none was a more tragic and dramatic figure than the "beauteous and gifted" Dora Hand. Appropriate to a subject worthy of grand opera, much of her life was shrouded in mystery and hearsay. She had been, according to one account, an operatic soprano in Boston when her career was interrupted by tuberculosis and she was forced to come west for her health. Another version credits an unhappy New England love affair for her escape to the anonymity of Dodge.

Facts later revealed that she was born Fannie Keenan, somewhere in the East, thirty-four years before she arrived in Dodge in 1877. She had married a Tin Pan Alley musician named Ted Hand, with whom she sang on the vaudeville circuit in the South and West between New Orleans and St. Louis. In St. Louis the act and marriage broke up, and Fannie teamed with another performer, Fannie Garretson, changing her first name to Dora to avoid confusion. As a veteran performer in the Southwest, Fannie Garretson had met and become a friend of James "Dog" Kelley and suggested to Dora that they try their luck in Dodge.

They were promptly engaged to perform at the Lady Gay dance hall and saloon, Bat Masterson's rowdy establishment on Front Street, which had billed such popular entertainers as Eddie Foy. Appearing as a soloist one evening, Dora was an instant hit; her "bell-like voice" appealed to untutored cowboys' ears as Jenny Lind's had captured the tough audiences of the Western mining towns. She also captivated Mayor Kelley, with whom she was later seen in intimate conclave, riding to Kelley's hounds or driving around the countryside in Kelley's four-in-hand.

Kelley was half owner with P. L. Beatty of the Alhambra, a competing saloon on Front Street. Using his influence as three-time mayor of Dodge City, Kelley arranged with the Lady Gay to allow Dora Hand to sing at the Alhambra as well, raising her salary to the astronomical figure of seventy-five dollars a week. Not only was Kelley seen often at the two saloons where Dora sang, but Dora herself was often seen going and coming from Kelley's three-room cabin on the fringes of the city.

Now began a strange chapter in Dora's life. In that city of little charity and less compassion the songstress began devoting all her spare time and money to helping the poor and less fortunate of Dodge. She became the town's "angel of mercy," distributing food to the impoverished, comfort to the sick, candy and toys to children. While the Methodists Ladies' Aid Society resented this woman from the wrong side of the tracks, the Reverend O. M. Wright invited her to appear as soloist at his Sunday-evening services. From then on Dora was alternately a disciple of the church and an idol of the dance halls and saloons.

That summer there appeared in Dodge a ne'er-do-well named James "Spike" Kenedy. Kenedy was the son of Mifflin Kenedy, part owner of the vast King Ranch of Texas and one of the wealthiest cattle barons in the West. Young Spike spent much of his time at the Alhambra, drinking up his father's money, until he became so drunk one night, and so attentive to Dora Hand, that Jim Kelley threw him out. Spike's injured pride demanded vengeance. Kelley would have to pay for this offense.

Spike's plan was simple: shoot Kelley while the latter was sleeping in his cabin, then escape to his father's ranch in Texas. He purchased a fast horse for his flight, then set a time for the assassination. The date, it so happened, fell during a week that Kelley was to be out of town on business; he had invited Fannie Garretson and Dora Hand to move into the cabin in his absence, as a pleasant change from their spartan quarters at the Lady Gay.

Spike Kenedy was unaware of this arrangement. Long after midnight on October 4 he crept up to the cabin, positioned himself at the window of Kelley's room, and fired four shots at the sleeping figure in the bed. One shot pierced Dora's side and killed her instantly. Satisfied that he'd slain the former mayor, Kenedy leaped on his horse and raced west along the Arkansas. His fleeing figure was identified, however, by Fannie Garretson and men in the Western Hotel who'd been awakened by the shots.

As the news of Dora's murder spread, Sheriff Bat Masterson organized a posse consisting of himself, deputy Bill Tilghman, ex-sheriff Charlie Bassett, and assistant city marshal Wyatt Earp. Bat reasoned that Kenedy's westward course was probably a ruse; that he would swing south toward his native Texas. In a driving blizzard of hail and rain, the four men rode to the Cimarron River and holed up at a likely spot where Kenedy might cross—staking everything on Bat's guess as to the route that Spike might follow.

That guess was right. Galloping on his lathered pony through the storm came Kenedy, confident of his escape. Only too late he saw the waiting figures on the riverbank. As he whirled his horse in a desperate effort to evade the trap, Bat fired, shattering his right arm. Spike kept on going till Wyatt Earp blasted his horse from under him. Easily overpowered, Kenedy at first was truculent; his killing of Kelley was fully justified by the latter's insult to his pride. Learning that he had murdered Dora Hand instead of Kelley, the fugitive was horrified; killing a woman was an unforgivable offense.

The posse returned to Dodge as the funeral for Dora Hand was taking place, the services solemnized by more genuine grief than the community had ever witnessed. Unfortunately present, "to pay their respects," were wealthy friends of Mifflin Kenedy. Now they insisted that the prisoner's arm be operated on to save it, a service performed by Dr. Tom McCarty, after which Spike was charged with murder. Twenty-four days later, he was tried behind closed doors in Sheriff Masterson's office, Judge R. G. Cook presiding. Surprisingly the verdict was: "Prisoner acquitted for lack of evidence to convict."

Needless to say, the decision raised a storm of protest in the city. It was widely believed, and correctly, that Mifflin Kenedy's cattle-baron friends had "dug deep in their pockets to save Spike." Kenedy's father arrived in time to whisk his son back to safety from the mob. But while Spike died three years later, Dora Hand lived on in affectionate memory in

Dodge, as "angel of mercy by day and honky-tonk singer after sundown."

If one tends to dwell on the dance-hall girls in the story of women in Dodge City, it is simply because they lived in the limelight of publicity and notoriety. But there were others, many of them, who simply performed the arduous duties of wife, mother, or sweetheart in a dangerous exacting life. They were a breed far different from their sisters of the tamed and civilized territories east of the Mississippi and Missouri rivers.

In the East where female frailty and delicate pursuits were a tradition, heroines like Molly Pitcher manning the guns at the battle of Monmouth or Sybil Ludington serving as female Paul Revere were immortalized in song and legend. But in the West the unsung heroines were legion. If a wagon train was attacked or a home besieged by Indians or outlaws, women were automatically given rifles to man the barricades beside their husbands. They faced danger and death as was expected of them, as Sybil Olds had done as she fought beside her husband in the Battle of Adobe Walls.

They had one reward and that was chivalrous respect. The toughest cowboy, gunman, or gambler doffed his hat to a lady on the wooden sidewalks and stepped aside to let her pass. An insult or coarse remark to a woman might lead to an instant challenge to a fistfight or a pistol duel. The stage performer Eddie Foy, arriving at Dodge in 1878, was surprised to note that in this rowdy and unruly town "a woman, no matter whether she was a housewife, a dance-hall girl, or even a courtesan—and mind you, the last two were not necessarily the same—was treated with grave courtesy on the street. Any man who failed to observe this canon got into trouble."

The last invasion of Dodge City by the fair sex took place in the latter days of its maturity when one Fred Harvey, an Eastern promoter, solved the problem of feeding transcontinental railroad passengers with a string of restaurants established at the wayside depots. He enlisted as waitresses (as his want ad read) "Young women of good character, attractive and intelligent, 18 to 30." Travelers accustomed to buying buffalo steaks from the open piles outside the depot, and having them cooked by the fireman on the train, found Harvey's food a pleasant innovation, while the waitresses inspired one traveler to poesy:

> Harvey Houses . . . on the Santa Fe
> They've strung 'em like a string of Indian beads;
> We all couldn't eat without 'em
> But the slickest thing about 'em
> Is the Harvey skirts that hustle up the feeds.

Travelers went so far as crediting Harvey with "civilizing the West." Certainly the disciplined, well-groomed ladies of impeccable character did much to set an example of good manners and decorum.

While the girls were under contract not to marry for a year, they were too rare an attraction at Dodge to keep potential husbands at a distance. It was estimated that throughout the West some five thousand Harvey girls married patrons of the Harvey restaurants, with four thousand babies christened Fred or Harvey in honor of the proprietor.

Which leads to a closing, appropriate note on motherhood. Heinie Schmidt, newspaper columnist in Dodge throughout its golden years, waxed eloquent on the subject: "All through the saga of the Plains there runs like a golden thread the memory of the pioneer mother. . . . Hers was the stirring articulate voice on the prairie and in the home over which she reigned in majestic grandeur, hovering over her brood in sunshine and in shadow. . . . In the sunset of life, the prairie conquered, her face radiant with happiness, she stands transfigured, a queen. The sod house a castle; the gingham, ermine; and the sunbonnet a crown."

A bit maudlin, perhaps, and expressed in truer but equally laudatory terms by a pioneer mother herself: "We did what we had to, we survived because we had to. There was never any choice."

9

To Hell on a Shutter

When Billy the Kid was a very young lad
  In Old Silver City he went to the bad;
Way out in the West with a gun in his hand
  At the age of twelve years he killed his first man.
Saga of Billy the Kid

Perhaps the most indelible picture of the Western cowtown, repeated so often in movies and television, is that of a wide street flanked by false-front dance halls and saloons. In the center of that street two men are stalking one another, grim and silent, hands hovering tensely over the six-guns on their hips. In doorways and windows and even on rooftops an expectant audience awaits that instant when guns are whipped from their holsters quicker than the eye can follow. Almost simultaneously four shots split the air and black smoke curls over the empty street. When the smoke clears, one man lies spreadeagled on his back, sightless eyes staring at the pitiless sun.

The scene played over and over again, in fiction
and on the screen, is not inaccurate. It was repeated
many times in Dodge, where the professional gunman, a term loosely applied to gunfighters outside
the law, was an ever present segment of the shifting
population. Their names were legion—Billy the Kid,
Clay Allison, Frank Leslie, John "Doc" Holliday, Ben
Thompson, and a score of others. So were the names
of their victims who were carried "to hell on a
shutter" to the graveyard on Boot Hill.

In Dodge, one man in his time played many parts.
The whole history of Kansas cowtowns, as one soon
discovers, presents the same characters in different
roles. Thus the gunman may become the gambler
and the gambler may become the marshal, until the
last discards his badge to become the outlaw once
again. To make clear distinctions is impossible. Bat
Masterson, Bill Hickok, even Wyatt Earp, were at
times outside the law—using their forty-fives for
personal gain or for settling a grudge.

In a study of the Western gunmen William Mac-
Leod Raine, who knew many of them personally,
puts them in three categories:

1. Those who were outright enemies of law and
order, who were dedicated to violence and even enjoyed taking human life—for example, Billy the Kid,
John Wesley Hardin, and Doc Holliday.

2. Those who generally remained within the law
and sometimes fought in behalf of it, though retain-

ing the right to use their guns in pursuit of personal interests. In this class were Wild Bill Hickok, Luke Short, and Bat Masterson.

3. Those who served society and never stepped beyond the boundaries of law enforcement. Billy Tilghman is cited as the principal example, a man who killed only in the interests of society, when he was forced to do so.

Considering the first variety, what caused these men to pursue what was, essentially, a life of crime? They might be cowboys trapped at the end of the line, for their useful years in the saddle were limited and, with no other skills, they were forced to live by the gun. Or they might be Confederate veterans seeking to keep alive their war against the North. They had learned to shoot and kill, and in a town like Dodge the enemy was ever present. Again, they might be homicidal maniacs, or men like Doc Holliday condemned to early death by tuberculosis and holding the lives of other men in little value.

Strangely enough, and this may apply to murderers in other areas, many had physical disabilities which might have caused them to take to the gun as a sort of recompense, to put themselves on a level with those not similarly handicapped.

Professional gunslingers were drawn to Dodge for the same reason that the town attracted gamblers, outlaws, rustlers, thieves, and ladies of easy virtue. Loose money abounded, and victims were plentiful.

A man could hire out his gun for a sizable fee, and when no assignment was forthcoming he could make a living at faro or poker, for fingers so expert on the trigger were adept at dealing aces from the bottom of the pack. It was even possible, in an emergency, that a deputy's badge would be pinned on his shirt, and he could earn money by turning on his own kind.

The gunman was essentially a loner. He had learned his trade by practice in the cowtowns that preceded Dodge as cattle centers, moving from place to place with the advancing railroad. Few knew where he really came from, or even what his true name was. But they had some features in common. According to one frontier reporter, "All had eyes either gray or blue, often a faded blue, expressionless, hard as jade." For whatever peculiar reason, the blue-eyed pattern seemed to hold true.

The only identification that a gunman carried with him, as he moved from town to town, was his record as a killer. His reputation preceded him, passing like wildfire down the chain of cowtowns strung along the Arkansas. Yet he was not regarded as a hunted criminal as long as he observed the gunman's code. If he was obliged to kill a man for professional reasons, he provoked a situation where they both met face to face and in the open, making sure his adversary was prepared and armed.

Then he relied on the advantage of the fast draw. If he killed his opponent with the first shot, and he often did, he was rarely convicted of murder or even brought to trial. For the gunman made sure there were ample witnesses to testify that it was a fair fight, "an exchange of shots," hence no one was to blame.

Though Billy the Kid was renowned as a killer, having shot his first man at the age of twelve, he was not the epitome of the professional gunman. He did not adhere to the gunman's code, requiring a face-to-face encounter under reasonably even odds. Billy shot from ambush, he shot in the back, he shot regardless of whether his victim had been properly forewarned and armed. By his twenty-first birthday, twenty-one men had died by his hand, one for each year of his murderous life. Appropriately, he was shot in the dark by a man he never saw, while visiting his Mexican girl friend in July 1881.

Who reigned supreme among the gunmen of the West? There was a wide choice. John Wesley Hardin, killer of thirty-five men before he had reached the age of twenty-five, was considered "one of the deadliest gunmen Texas ever produced." Doc Holliday was hailed as "the coldest-blooded killer east of the Rockies." Bat Masterson, himself at times a gunman, considered Ben Thompson "the most dangerous killer in the West," a hackneyed phrase that was sometimes applied by the Kansas press to Bat himself.

Ben Thompson, born of English parents who had moved to Texas, first tested his skill at age thirteen

by firing mustard seed into the buttocks of his playmates. He was pardoned by the local judge because
of his obvious sympathy for the suffering of his companions. From that point on, according to his biographer, Thompson's forty-one-year career on earth
"gurgles like a blood-bath."

Ben was short and stocky for a gunman, five feet
seven, swarthy and dark haired with the proverbial
slate-blue eyes. He had served long enough in the
Confederate army to be thrown into the guardhouse
for shooting his sergeant. Though chained to the
floor, Ben had managed to set his jail afire and
escaped in the confusion to renew his war against
society. As an itinerant gambler in Southwestern frontier towns, he featured in one fight after another,
with army officers being his favorite targets. After
killing two more sergeants, he was again thrown into
chains and pinned on his back to the ground, remaining in that position for a month.

The chastisement had little effect. On his release
Ben joined his younger brother Billy in Abilene,
where the latter was punching cows by day and
gambling by night. Together they ran the gambling
tables at the Bull's Head Tavern, from which em-
porium Ben virtually ruled the town. Few questioned
his gun-imposed authority. When hauled into court
for one of the many shootouts at the Bull's Head,
Ben turned his gun on the judge and ordered him
off the bench.

"Don't ever let me catch you playing at being judge again," he told the magistrate. "If I do, you're as good as dead."

It was at Ellsworth that Ben was pitted against Wyatt Earp. Brother Billy had killed Sheriff Chauncey B. Whitney in a street altercation. Some claimed the shooting was an accident, but others heard Billy saying, "I'd have shot the marshal if he was Jesus Christ." In any event Ben and a band of twenty-five armed followers kept the authorities at bay until Billy made good his escape. At that point Ben found himself confronting Wyatt Earp, the latter suddenly presented with a marshal's badge by Mayor James Miller.

The confrontation was a classic example of deadly gunman facing an equally deadly frontier lawman. Each knew the other by sight and reputation. It was as much a duel of nerves as of weapons. Wyatt himself reported:

> All I had to do was keep my eyes on Ben's shotgun . . . [and] on the target I had picked, his stomach just back of his hand. I figured he'd wait for me to get within thirty or forty yards to make his weapon most effective and that he could not get his shotgun into action without "telegraphing the move" . . . through his wrist. When I saw his wrist move to put his arm muscles into play, I'd go for my guns, and I had enough confidence in myself to be certain that I could put at least one slug into his belly before he could pull a trigger.

As they closed in, with only forty yards between them, Thompson called out:

"What do you figure on doing, Wyatt?"

"I'm either killing you or taking you to jail," said Earp.

Ben halted momentarily, and with that hesitation Wyatt knew he could take him, alive or dead.

"Come on, throw down your gun or make your fight," he ordered.

Surprisingly, Thompson grinned, threw down his shotgun, and dropped his revolver belt beside it. As Ben confessed, he was both a fatalist and a realist: willing to face death when the odds were even, but not a candidate for suicide.

Perhaps it is not surprising that the careers of the great gunslingers of that era are related to that of Wyatt Earp. As marshal he was the natural enemy; as skilled gunfighter he was a challenging target. Shoot the marshal and one's reputation soared. Be beaten or outsmarted by him and no great shame ensued.

Oddly enough, and perhaps out of mutual respect, many professional gunmen sided at one time or another with the lawmen they tangled with. A few years after the above encounter Thompson was in Dodge when Earp was serving as assistant marshal. All differences between them were ignored; and when Thompson learned of a plot to ambush Earp he probably saved the marshal's life by warning him of the plan. Similarly, when Bat Masterson shot army sergeant Melvin King in Sweetwater, Thompson—who seems to have been everywhere in those days—appeared suddenly with his shotgun and kept the authorities from nailing Bat before he made his getaway.

Discounting his fleeting virtues, Thompson, perhaps more than anyone, typified the Western gunman of that era—not only because of his nervy skill with a six-gun but, as one contemporary put it, because of "his craving to kill people." The Thompson brothers together were rumored to have sent fifty men to hell on a shutter. The authentic figures list twenty-seven slayings, only two by Billy and the rest by Ben. Both died, as they lived, by the gun—Ben being shot some ten years later in a pistol fight in Austin (it took nine bullets to bring him down), the fugitive Billy reported as being "killed in Indian Territory."

Rivaling Ben Thompson as arch gunman of the West was Tennessee-born Clay Allison. Their life spans were about the same, even their careers were similar. Like Thompson, Allison had been a Confederate private in the Civil War and spent most of his time in the guardhouse for shooting an officer. But, apart from their "gunman's eyes," they differed in appearance. Six feet two, weighing 175 pounds, Allison was described as having "black hair, blue eyes . . . a determined mouth and a bewhiskered chin." When sober, he was quiet, unassuming, even courtly; but he was very rarely sober.

Like Thompson he learned to handle guns in childhood, but instead of shooting his playmates he accidentally shot himself in the foot, acquiring a permanent limp. His biographer suggests that "that physical defect may have forced him to seek compensation in firearms and to take seriously any remarks which seemed to be veiled slights."

The point seems valid. One of his earlier victims was a gun-toting cowhand named Buck Bowman, whose scathing remarks regarding Clay reached Allison's ears.

Clay sought out Buck and introduced himself. In his courteous Southern speech, he said, "I hear you-all got a big mouth." With which, according to one account:

> He backed off five short steps. Then Bowman crouched, his elbows crooked, and both clawed hands streaked for leather. Allison's gun hand blurred—the big Navy Colt bucked and roared. The heavy wallop of the .45 slug spun Bowman clear round. His guns spanged a vicious echo, and dust sprayed Clay's boots. But it was the reflex act of a dead man.

Sober, Allison was a pleasant, agreeable fellow, and the law made allowance for his infirmity. On entering town it was Clay's playful habit to ride down Main Street, blasting his guns and shouting: "All lights out!" Riding back again, he shot out those that weren't extinguished, whether on the streets or in the buildings. Playfully firing holes through the hat of a local doctor, he promptly bought the man a new hat when he learned of his profession.

Yet there was no getting around it: Clay was an impulsive murderer. On one occasion, drinking at a bar, three black soldiers in Union uniforms entered the saloon. All three were shot dead in an instant, Clay confessing that he was simply acting on his Southern prejudice. Dining at a restaurant, he saw at an adjoining table a Mexican who had once bad-mouthed the gunman. Without leaving his chair, Clay shot the Mexican through the head, then went on eating.

Saloonkeepers dreaded his presence; Clay drunk was literally murder. Not daring to refuse him service, they plied him with drinks on the house until he passed out, then dragged him out and tied him across the saddle of his pony, and let the pony carry him home

On arriving at Dodge, Clay checked in at the Wright House and limped into the bar, taking a stool beside an Easterner named Bennington DuPont who was helping himself to doughnuts from the free lunch bowl. "Pardner," said Clay politely, in his faltering speech, "please pass the fried holes." Unaware of the gunman's identity, DuPont made a fatal error.

"You know," he said, "you limp in your talk as you do in your walk." In an instant Clay's guns were pointed at DuPont's forehead. "Either draw your guns, varmint, or get out of town—fast." DuPont got out of town fast and never returned.

Told of the incident, Sheriff Bat Masterson, who was troubled by Allison's presence in Dodge, conceded that perhaps Clay had done the town a favor by ridding it of one more undesirable Eastern dude. However, he suggested that Clay leave town. The suggestion was expectedly resented. Clay did leave town, but only briefly. When he returned it was with a band of wealthy Texas cattlemen, who had persuaded Clay to try for the thousand-dollar bounty offered for shooting Marshal Wyatt Earp. They had agreed to stand by and back him up as needed.

There are many versions of what happened next, but all conform to the classic pattern of the gun-slinging killer suddenly confronted by a man like Wyatt Earp. Bat Masterson warned Wyatt of Clay's intent while the marshal was breakfasting at the Dodge House. "I can take Allison," said Wyatt calmly, continuing his breakfast.

"Sure you can," said Bat. "But he's got a dozen Texas cowboys here to back him up. They'll be ready to take you if Allison doesn't."

Wyatt applied some practical psychology. If Clay was outside and waiting for him, let him wait. Every minute of stewing in his own juice would add to the gunman's nervous impatience, make him tense and edgy and less confident. The marshal delayed over extra cups of coffee, then went upstairs to shave and dress with slow deliberation, while Clay darted back and forth through the batwing doors of the Long Branch for drinks to steady his nerves. Then Wyatt lit a cigar, and strode casually out the door to confront the waiting killer. They exchanged four words.

"You Earp?" asked Clay.

"I'm Earp," said Wyatt, walking directly up to Allison until they stood almost hip to hip.

"Clay was working for his gun all the time," said Wyatt later, "trying to get into such a position that I couldn't see him reach for it."

Things moved so fast that the watchers on the street were scarcely aware of what happened. Clay whipped his gun out of its holster, his finger on the hammer, when the scowl on his face dissolved into astonishment. His gun dropped as if it had suddenly turned red-hot and scorched his hand. For before he had had a firm grip on the butt, the barrel of Wyatt's forty-five was buried three inches in the softness of his belly.

"Get out of town," said Wyatt. "Don't come back."

Those in the Long Branch witnessed the scrubby end to Allison's career in Kansas. Clay leaped on his horse, and dashed in the opposite direction. As he passed Wright's store where his Texas supporters had been watching, he screamed, "You sneaking coyotes, a hell of a backing-up job you did!"

If too often repeated, the stories and legends of

the cowtown gunmen acquire a dreary sameness. Even phrases like "ruthless killer," "lightning-like draw," and "nerves of steel" lose significance by repetition. The same applies to lawman turned gunman, of which there are innumerable, sometimes tiresome examples—tiresome, that is, except to those who never were sure when the man behind the badge might change to killer.

Doc Holliday was more of a gun-toting, gambling desperado than he was a dentist. Like Thompson he had been a teenage killer, shooting two black youths in Georgia who had trespassed on his swimming hole. While he befriended and even aided certain lawmen like Wyatt Earp, the duties of law enforcement were too tame to tempt him. Wrote Stuart Lake, who interviewed many Dodge City characters:

> Doc Holliday was a hot-headed, ill-tempered, trouble-hunting and, withal, cold-blooded desperado, rightly placed by history in the gunman-killer category of Ben Thompson, John Wesley Hardin, and Clay Allison. He was no sooner out of one scrape than he was into another, and was greatly feared and genuinely disliked by all except a very few who knew him.

According to Wyatt Earp himself there was only one man in the West, Frank Leslie of Tombstone, who could match Doc's quickness on the draw. But, Wyatt observed, "Leslie lacked Doc's fatalistic courage, induced, I suppose, by the nature of Holliday's disease—tuberculosis—and the realization that he hadn't long to live, anyway. That fatalism, coupled with his marvelous speed and accuracy, gave Holliday the edge over any out-and-out killer I ever knew."

Shortly after Earp's battle with the Driscoll gang in the winter of 1879, as related later, Wyatt left for Tombstone, Arizona. He had tamed Dodge City. Now the burgeoning mining camp, the "Howling Wonder of the Western World," was where the action was. Gunfights and killings were everyday occurrences and the motto of "a man for breakfast" was transferred like a signboard from Dodge City to the silver-plated streets of Tombstone. The town engaged Wyatt's services as marshal.

Doc Holliday followed Earp to Arizona to escape the irascible Big Nose Kate, adding three gunfight victims to his record on the way. But Kate caught up with her fugitive husband, and in the manner of a woman scorned she fingered Doc as one of the outlaws who had held up an east-west stagecoach, killing the driver and making off with eighty thousand dollars.

Doc indignantly denied the charge in court, explaining to the judge that the holdup was not on a par with his professional capacities. Had he been involved, he would have shot the horses, not the driver, making things easy for himself. The judge accepted this reasoning and dismissed the case but, with suspicion still hanging over him, Doc offered to leave Tombstone lest he embarrass his good friend Wyatt Earp.

"Don't *you* leave town," said Wyatt. "Just get rid of that crazy wife of yours."

The marshal lent Doc a thousand dollars, with which the latter bribed Kate to leave Arizona, and Doc Holliday, for good. It successfully ended their marathon matrimonial battle.

Doc's last big gunfight occurred at Tombstone in October 1881. The town was being terrorized by a band of renegade cowboys headed by the Clanton brothers, Ike and Billy, the McLowery brothers, Frank and Tom, and a professional gunman named Billy Claiborne. Some three hundred cowboys sided with this tough quintet in defying the lawmen of the town, the latter consisting of Wyatt, Virgil, and Morgan Earp, and, as temporary deputy, Doc Holliday.

Both Doc and Wyatt refused to be intimidated by the gang. They repeatedly roughed up the Clanton and McLowery brothers and finally pitched them into jail. However, they were promptly released by County Sheriff Johnny Behan, who found it expedient to pander to the outlaws. This encouraged the cowboys to call for a showdown. They holed up behind the adobe walls of the O.K. Corral, commanding the center of the town, and challenged the Earps and Holliday to come and get them.

At high noon of October 26 the siege of the O.K.

Corral began. The quartet of marshals descended on the outpost in formation, like a drill squad on parade. The resulting battle was decided in exactly fifteen seconds. The cowboys opened fire first, slightly wounding Virgil Earp. The attackers paused, took careful aim, and pinpointed their targets with a hail of lead.

Wyatt drilled Frank McLowery through the stomach; Morgan shattered Billy Clanton's gun hand, putting him out of commission; Doc Holliday with his nickel-plated Colt sent three slugs through Tom McLowery's stomach and another through the wounded Frank McLowery's heart. Ike Clanton and Billy Claiborne fled for shelter and, to Doc's disgust, were captured unharmed. Doc was not one for taking prisoners alive.

In the complex maneuvering of frontier justice, Sheriff Behan charged the city marshals and Doc Holliday with murder.

"Arrest us!" shouted Wyatt Earp. "Don't you or any of your lackeys try it!"

The fight at the O.K. Corral, which concerns more the history of Tombstone than of Dodge, was practically Doc's swan song as an itchy gunman. Two years later he reappeared in Dodge with the three Earp brothers in what might be called the Second Battle for Dodge City. But no further killings were linked to his name. Perhaps Doc was subdued by the shadow of approaching death. Three years later he lost the greatest battle of his lifetime with tuberculosis.

But the sound of bullets still echoed over Dodge, where every other man who carried firearms was a potential gunman. Rivalries and jealousies exploded like dynamite at the slightest provocation. A casual insult, an unintended slight, an accidental misdeal in a game of cards, and one or more victims in the line of fire were carried to Doc McCarty's office or to Ham Bell's funeral home.

Typical of those unscheduled and impromptu fights was one that took place in April 1879. Reported the Dodge City *Globe:* "There is seldom witnessed in any civilized town or country such a scene as transpired at the Long Branch Saloon last Saturday evening, resulting in the killing of Levi Richardson, a well-known fighter, by a gambler named Frank Loving."

It was believed that both were rivals for the favors of a dance-hall girl, but the actual shooting started with a brief exchange of words. Said Loving, "You're not man enough to fight." Said Richardson, "Try me and see." Immediately, with the barrels of their pistols almost touching, eleven shots were fired, five by Richardson and six by Loving. Strangely enough, even at point-blank range, Loving remained unscathed though Richardson was riddled with bullets, dying almost instantly. Loving escaped trial for murder on a plea of self-defense, standard procedure in Dodge City gunfights.

Neither man had been entitled to carry arms in the Long Branch, or any place north of the Dead Line, but the editor of the *Globe* noted extenuating circumstances: "Gamblers, as a class, are desperate men. They consider it necessary in their business that they keep up their fighting reputation, and never take a bluff. On no account should they be allowed to carry deadly weapons." Sound advice—but, like so much sound advice on the frontier, impossible to implement.

Unlike those who fought with guns within the law, the gunman died with his boots on, generally at an early age, following the fate of Billy the Kid, gunned down at twenty-seven. His coffin was a plain pine box, his shroud was a saddle blanket, and the evasive words on his tombstone told their story: "Died of Lead Poisoning," or "Killed by Lightning." Many lived on in legend; but it was hard to justify their lives on moral grounds—unless one forgives the code they lived by. That code, briefly stated: kill or be killed. Once the gunman obeyed the first of these commands, the second was foreordained—and he kept on killing, since a man condemned to death has nothing left to lose.

10

Lady Luck and Her Disciples

Dodge City, then, was the end of the trail,
Where gamblers were ready to lift your bale;
They knew how to stack and they knew how to deal,
And they knew how to spin a fortune wheel.
Texas Trail to Dodge City

The sign read: ONLY LEGITIMATE GAMBLING PER-
MITTED. It was posted prominently on Dodge City's
Front Street; and it stayed there while the wheels
spun and the dice rolled and the cards were dealt in
virtually every bar and place of entertainment on the
Plaza.

The notice was not intended to discourage gambling. It was only a warning to those who might
disrupt its free and orderly operation. For games of
chance, far from being considered a vice or even a
misdemeanor in Dodge, were the life's blood of the
city, like the cattle trade which kept it going. It not
only lured the Texas cattlemen and other visitors to

Dodge, it kept a large part of their money there—to the benefit of the merchant, the saloon and dance-hall owners, and the town officials whose salaries were paid by the ten-dollar tax, or "fine," on gambling operators.

The term "legitimate" on the Front Street sign was meant to outlaw the crooked gambling devices that were common in the early days of Dodge. Since the Plaza was public domain and a part of the Santa Fe Trail, which bisected the city, it was the perfect trap for the cowboy with four to six months' wages in his pocket who saw no point in taking all that money back to Texas. The card sharp and the shell-game operator, working on the principle that the hand is quicker than the eye, helped to solve the cowboy's problem. He rarely had money left to take back to the Lone Star State.

In particular disrepute were the so-called show-case games, or crooked lotteries conducted on the Plaza. A temporary booth was erected on the square, in which were temptingly displayed assorted jewelry and exotic furbelows, gold rings and diamond stick pins, silver watches, ivory-handled knives, and other gewgaws. "You picks your number and you takes your choice." That the winning number was rarely chosen was the obvious secret of the operator's profit.

When Jim "Dog" Kelley became mayor, the show-case games were marked for doom. An arrogant promoter defied Marshal Larry Deger's order to

move on, and insisted on his right to operate under
the sanction of free enterprise. Deger, in what for
him was a rare display of spirit, picked up the display case and hurled it to the street, shattering the
glass and scattering the prizes far and wide. A general melee ensued in which everybody helped himself to treasure trove. As a consequence, the local
press reported, "The 'jeweler' has gone. Before leaving, his physical features were greatly changed, a
phenomenon which he will doubtless explain to his
friends in the East as a sample of the strange ways
of the Far West. In the process he is said to have
swallowed several teeth."

Virtually every saloon and dance hall had its card
tables or gaming rooms in which the prospective
gambler could find anything from roulette and dice
to poker games with thousand-dollar stakes. Even in
the Comique Theater, attention was split between
the vaudeville performance on the platform and the
action at the gaming tables. Eddie Foy described
this feature of the Western music hall:

> The songs and patter from the stage at one end;
> the click and clatter of poker chips, balls, cards,
> dice, wheels and other devices at the other end,
> mingled with a medley of crisp phrases—"Thirty-five
> to one!" "Get your money down, folks!" "Eight to
> one on the colors." "Keno!" "Are you all down,
> gentlemen?"

In the complex pattern of the frontier cowtown
it was not unusual to see the city marshal or his

deputies running gambling parlors, just as they ran saloons and dance halls and even less savory establishments. In fact it made good sense. In that quarrelsome fraternity, where tempers were short and tension high, it was wise to have a banker or a dealer who was fast and handy with a gun. Bat Masterson, Bill Tilghman, Larry Deger, Wyatt Earp, along with others, were all at one time owners or part owners of a gambling operation, generally coupled with a dance hall or saloon.

Far from distracting from the lawmen's reputation, it enhanced it. "Gambling," said Bat Masterson, "was not only the principal and best paying industry in town but was also reckoned among its most respectable." Erstwhile mayors of the city such as P. L. Beatty, George Hoover, and Jim Kelley were inveterate promoters of the game, while officers Masterson and Wyatt Earp, though they often gambled from Saturday's dusk to dawn, were deacons of Reverend Wright's church on Sunday.

Poker—in its rudimentary form of five cards dealt to each player and the highest combination winning —was the universal game. Keno, similar to bingo, was also popular. Chuck-a-luck, in which three dice were shuffled in a cage, paid winner's odds of 180 to one if all three showed the same array of dots. The roulette wheel, with thirty-two red and black numbered compartments in which the spinning ball might come to rest, paid odds of up to thirty-two to one, with proportionate losses. Faro, in which the players bet on the sequence of cards drawn face up from the pack, with the banker, or dealer, playing against the field, was the favorite game of the professionals.

While the professional gambler was a breed apart and sometimes regarded with suspicion, he also attracted players to his table by the challenge of his reputation—just as the professional gunman tempted others to test their skill against his reputed expertise. According to Dodge City chronicler Stanley Vestal, "A gambler's career usually fell into this pattern: first, a killing in self-defense; then a job as a gunman and bouncer in a gambling house; then a position as gambler playing on a percentage for the house; later, a partnership in or ownership of a dance hall, saloon, or other gambling place; and finally—on attaining years of discretion—a move to some safer place and job."

Though the gambler's dress of black frock coat, white shirt, and string tie was a self-declaring trademark, there were those who saw an advantage in disguising their profession. One successful operator appeared in Dodge in the clerical garb of a Presbyterian minister. Gambling, he told the players in the Lady Gay, was God's method of rewarding the deserving and the virtuous and punishing the sinners. Before each game he invited the others to join him in prayer. Finally detected with an ace up his sleeve, he pronounced the discovery a miracle. Only God could have put it there.

The patrons of the Lady Gay recalled with chagrin the innocent-looking rube with farm-boy clothes and manners who shyly inquired of Jim Kelley, "Do they ever play poker around here?" Yes, Kelley told him, "but stay away from these sharks, they'll strip you clean." The sharks, however, were eager to accommodate the greenhorn—especially when the lad announced that, though he had some money, he knew hardly anything about the game. In fact he even asked for instructions on how to shuffle and deal the cards.

Of course, as it turned out, the "greenhorn," to his professed surprise, won pot after pot until he had cleaned out every other player at the table. "We tried every trick in the book," one of his victims confessed, "marked cards, extra aces, dealing from the bottom of the pack, but nothing stopped him." Said Kelley with amused philosophy, "That green-looking kid sure taught the town a lesson. As Mark Twain said, you can't tell how far a frog can jump by looking at him."

Cheating, or the ever-present suspicion of cheating, was a constant source of gunplay in the gambling saloons. One resourceful mountebank with an ace secreted up his sleeve found himself in danger of exposure. Ordering a sandwich from the bar, he slipped the incriminating card between its slices and innocently ate it. Apparently the ruse did not go undetected. For ever after, the slippery gentleman was known as "Eat 'Em Up Jake."

Sheer bravery sometimes avoided bloodshed. An English visitor once accused Ben Thompson, one of the deadliest of gunmen, of cheating in a card game. Ben whipped out his forty-four and covered him. "Take it back—and quick!" commanded Ben. The Englishman glared into the barrel of the gun as if to stare it down. "Shoot and be damned. I say you cheat," he shouted. In admiration of the Briton's nerve, Ben lowered his gun and laughed—suggesting merely that the visitor leave the game if he questioned its propriety.

More than one citizen of the early Southwest made a handsome living at the gaming tables, and sooner or later the vast majority ended up in Dodge. If one were to choose a representative of this fraternity, Luke Short would be a good selection. Born on his father's ranch in western Texas in 1854, Luke had so little education that he could barely sign his own name. At an early age he started trading with the Indians, a gallon of homemade "Pine Top Whiskey" worth ninety cents for a buffalo robe worth ten times that amount. The deal sent too many drunken Indians on the rampage, and a corps of United States Cavalry was dispatched to arrest the youngster. They caught up with Luke all right, but the latter looked so innocent that they let him escape to Colorado.

In the mining town of Leadville, Luke was introduced to faro, and became addicted to the game. At this point it was noticed that he "wore a seven-and-one-eighth size hat, denoting a native, shrewd intelligence." But he had yet to qualify as a gunman, so essential to one's standing as a gambler. The chance came when a hard-boiled miner challenged one of Luke's bets. Luke slipped out his gun and drilled the miner through the cheek.

This incident raised him to the rank of the professionals; he began roving the mining camps and Kansas cowtowns as a faro dealer. Proprietors of gambling parlors hired Luke to sit at their tables, knowing his very presence would intimidate the crooked players. Yet when he showed up in Dodge in 1876 his baby-faced appearance belied his double role of gambler and gunman. "Mr. Short is a quiet unassuming person," a local editor reported. "It is hard to believe him the red-handed desperado which the Dodge mob pictures him to be." The writer went on:

> He is a man rather under medium height, but well built and firmly knit, with nothing in his features to indicate irregular or dissipated habits. He is cleanly-shaved, excepting only a natty little mustache, and is dressed with great care and in good style. He sports a magnificent diamond pin, and yesterday twirled

between his fingers an elegant black walking stick with a gold head . . . there is no doubt that he is able to take care of himself in almost any kind of crowd.

For two years Luke handled the gambling concession at the Long Branch, then owned by Chalkley Beeson and Will Harris. Here he became good friends with Masterson and Wyatt Earp. In fact, the trio became something of a three-man team in big-league gambling. Short followed Masterson and Earp to Tombstone, which by 1880 was becoming a sanctuary for many gunslinging characters who had worn out their welcome in Dodge City. At Tombstone he dealt faro for Wyatt Earp in the latter's busy Oriental Saloon and Gambling Hall. Here, in a shooting fray, Luke enhanced his reputation by ridding the town of one of its more obnoxious six-gun artists, Charlie Storms.

This combination of killer and gambler, seemingly inseparable, is better personified, however, by Doc Holliday. His career as gunman is noted elsewhere. But both his reputation and his record as a gambler were extraordinary. According to Wyatt Earp, the only man who was reasonably close to Holliday, "Doc was the nerviest, most skillful gambler that I ever knew. I have seen him bet ten thousand dollars on the turn of a card."

Some thought it was unrequited love that turned Doc's life into a marathon of drink and gambling.

Forced west for his health and doomed to die of tuberculosis, he could not forget the girl he left behind him. By the time he reached Dodge, confirmed in his unrighteous path at the age of twenty-six, he had not seen Mattie for seven years. Wrote Doc's biographer:

> The cruelest and dearest vision of his lonely night was her face. He was barred from her society forever, an outcast, despised, something no decent woman would speak to. . . . He would reach for the bottle beside his bed and drink until the sharp sword of his thoughts melted into soft and formless clouds. The next day he would force the sick heart numb by concentrating on the cards, the opium of his days.

It was true that Doc drank prodigiously. "Two and three quarts of liquor a day was not unusual for him," remembered Wyatt Earp, yet Wyatt added that he had never seen Doc intoxicated. And once Holliday sat down at the poker table, "his eyes saw everything and could get a look in them that chilled off any desire to get funny." In a card game Doc was literally murder. Once, in Denver, he was forced to check his guns at the entrance to a gambling house. But just for such contingencies he carried a knife slung on a cord around his neck. Bud Ryan, a local gambler, tried to cheat Doc in a faro game, and when Doc challenged him, Ryan went for a gun concealed inside his belt. Doc beat him to the action with his knife, and slashed the gambler horribly, scarring him for life.

Like many gamblers who lived exclusively by cards, Doc Holliday had few friends. Bat Masterson distrusted him; Ben Thompson, when gambling at the Long Branch, refused to drink with him at the bar—a form of social ostracism. Only Wyatt Earp was tolerant of "his undeniably poor disposition." Though Big Nose Kate kept a hawklike eye on Doc, he spent their married life trying to break the bond, and finally succeeded. "As far as the world in general was concerned," wrote Wyatt Earp, "there was nothing in his soul but iron."

Ben Thompson was another gunman-gambler bent on fleecing the human race. Ben had become addicted to gambling as a way of life while a printer's devil in New Orleans, where he supplemented his meager income by playing roulette, faro, monte, poker, or any other game available. From then on, it was reported, "he always relied upon his skill as applied to the laws of luck and chance."

After touring the Southwestern gambling towns, Ben teamed for a while with Phil Coe, another inveterate gambler, in Abilene. Coe was killed by Wild Bill Hickok in a shooting fray in one of Abilene's gaming houses, and Ben moved on to Ellsworth, where he and his brother Billy ran the gambling at the Bull's Head Tavern. When Billy became a fugitive after killing Sheriff Chauncey Whitney, Ben came to

Dodge and holed up at the Long Branch, where he became an institutional figure like Luke Short. However, Ben and Luke were kept apart at separate tables; their gambling skills were so closely matched as to make them dangerous to one another.

Thompson was no better liked in Dodge than Holliday, except by Bat Masterson, who admired his skill with guns as well as with cards. He himself respected only nerve and courage, as he'd shown toward the Englishman who had called him down for cheating. For some reason or other he bore a grudge against the mild-mannered Eddie Foy who was performing at the Comique Theater—perhaps, Eddie believed, because he knew that Foy disliked him. He stumbled drunkenly into Eddie's dressing room one night, while the comedian was applying make-up by the light of an oil lamp standing just beside him.

"Getcher head outa the way!" said Thompson. "I aim to shoot out that light."

Then, as Eddie Foy recorded in his memoirs:

> I was seized with a sudden foolish obstinacy. I wasn't going to move my head just because a drunken bum like Thompson wanted to shoot out a lamp. . . . I just sat there staring at him as impudently as I could . . . then Bat Masterson burst into the scene, threw the muzzle of Thompson's gun upward, and partly by coaxing, partly by shoving, got him out. When they had gone, I found my hands shaking so that I couldn't put on my make-up.

Why he didn't shoot, I don't know. He didn't mind taking life; he'd killed no telling how many men, and was drunk enough at that moment to be absolutely reckless. But perhaps I was rather small game for him. A man accustomed to killing tigers would feel himself belittled if he were asked to go on a squirrel hunt.

Eddie Foy himself wasn't much of a gambler, but he had learned from simple observation the value of the blank-faced bluff.

To depict all cowtown gamblers as gunmen on the one hand, or tenderfoot dupes on the other, is extreme. Men of respectable positions in Dodge City gambled extensively, and the local press reported their winnings and losses as the *Wall Street Journal* might report stock-market trends. When the ex-governor of Kansas, Thomas Carney, visited Dodge in 1877, ostensibly to canvass his chances for reelection, it became quickly apparent that his aim was gambling. As the Dodge City *Times* reported, "The Governor's reputation and dignified bearing soon enabled him to decoy four of our business men into a social game of poker. . . . One of Governor Carney's intended victims was Colonel Charles Norton, wholesale dealer and financial operator."

The game proceeded along normal channels, until the classic confrontation came. Governor Carney drew four kings, a seemingly unbeatable hand. Colonel Norton opened the pot with a hundred-dollar bill and the governor raised him while the other two players dropped out. Carney and Norton kept raising the ante, each believing the other was bluffing, until the governor was forced to contribute his gold watch and chain and all his personal possessions to the pot. Then the moment came to show his hand.

A breathless silence pervaded the room as Governor Carney spread his four kings on the table, and affectionately encircled the glittering heap of gold, silver, greenbacks and precious stones with his arm, preparatory to raking in the spoils. But at that moment a sight met the old Governor's gaze which caused his eyes to dilate with horror. Right in front of Colonel Norton were spread four genuine and perfectly formed aces. . . .

The next eastward bound freight train carried an old man, without shirt studs or other ornament, apparently bowed down by overwhelming grief, and the trainman hadn't the heart to throw him overboard. Governor Carney is not visiting this city on business any more.

"Gambling was better last week than it has been in Dodge for many a day," blithely announced a reporter the next morning, predicting a promising future for the gambling establishments. Yes, Lady Luck was the city's mistress throughout all her tempestuous and prosperous career.

11

Doctors in Ten-gallon Hats

And there is the doctor, I like to forgot,
I believe to my soul he's the worst of the lot.
He'll tell you he'll cure you for half you possess,
And when you're buried he'll take all the rest.
                              Hard Times

Shortly after arriving and setting up practice in Dodge City, Dr. Samuel Crumbine was fetched to attend a rancher thirty miles outside of town. The patient had suffered a broken leg in an argument with a bronco. Crumbine applied the necessary bandages and splints with the aid of the rancher's foreman, then prepared to leave.

"You stay here!" the rancher ordered, and, on signal, the foreman blocked the doorway with his Springfield rifle.

"I've got patients in town," protested Crumbine. "I'll be back tomorrow."

"Unless you remain here," said the rancher grimly, "you'll be dead tomorrow."

Needless to say, the young doctor stayed until the leg showed signs of healing—earning a handsome fee and also learning an invaluable lesson. On the frontier a doctor had to yield to circumstances, extraordinary as those circumstances often were.

Setting a fractured limb at gunpoint, extracting a bullet by the light of a single candle shakily held by the patient himself, performing kitchen surgery on a rickety table with no assistance, covering scores of miles by horse or buggy in all kinds of weather— these were only a few of the frontier doctor's hardships. An even greater handicap was ignorance—his own, admitted, and that of his stubborn, often superstitious patients.

On the Plains the scout and traveler, hunter and cowboy, tended, with inherent self-reliance, to treat his own illnesses and injuries. For this he depended on folklore, native herbs and superstitions, and even on his hunting knife for self-administered surgery. More than once the young Kit Carson, veteran trailman of the Santa Fe, was called upon to amputate a gangrened leg or arm with a buffalo knife and carpenter's saw, relying on whiskey as an anesthetic and guided only by his common sense and crude experience.

Indian nostrums peddled on the streets of Dodge by itinerant, self-styled "doctors" sold like hotcakes.

They cured every known ailment from indigestion and aching muscles to cholera and smallpox—not to mention typhoid, frostbite, and tuberculosis. Most popular, perhaps, was Dr. Johnson's Indian Blood Syrup, "the best remedy known to man." Johnson, the label stated, had learned its secret formula as a prisoner of the Comanches. Heavily loaded with alcohol or opium, or both, such nostrums produced an instant euphoria as proof of their effectiveness. If a patient subsequently suffered from their aftereffects, or even died, the peripatetic doctor was long gone before these sad results became apparent.

But the legitimate physician, he who came to towns like Dodge with honest purpose, was one of the unsung heroes of the frontier. He brought little with him beyond his instrument bag, his courage, and a minimum of schooling—that minimum being the best that he could get. The few medical schools existing in the East (there were none whatever west of the Mississippi) offered nothing like the rigorous training of today. A prospective doctor might first get a job with the local druggist, grinding powders, compounding formulas, preparing tinctures, pills, elixirs, plasters.

After this preliminary training he would "intern" as assistant to the local doctor, reading medicine as fledgling lawyers would "read" law with a local, practicing attorney. He would accompany the doctor on his daily rounds, assisting in minor operations, applying poultices, bandages, and dressings, administering anesthetics, making himself useful as the case demanded.

During this period he observed and absorbed his tutor's methods of amputating a limb, sewing up a wound, delivering a baby, or extracting a bullet—until he felt qualified to perform these tasks himself. At that point, with a pocket surgical kit and stethoscope, he was ready to hang out his shingle. In a frontier town like Dodge he might initiate or expand his practice by buying or establishing a drugstore, consulting his patients over the counter, and reaching to the shelves behind to supply the cure.

Ill trained because of circumstances, he learned by doing. "A doctor learns medicine," wrote the frontier physician Arthur Hertzler, "just as an Indian learns to track—that is, by tracking." Hertzler himself reported that in one twenty-four-hour period he examined forty patients in his "office" and traveled sixty miles by buggy to make house calls.

The doctor's office was often his one-room living quarters, with a single chair and an examination or operating table he had built himself. But most of his surgery was performed in the primitive kitchens of his patients. Here he observed no such refinements as sterilized gowns and masks and rubber gloves. The surgeon simply washed his hands at the pump and boiled his instruments in the family dishpan. And of course there were no nurses or assistants.

There were apt to be, however, plenty of curious would-be witnesses, and the doctor usually covered the windows with sheets to keep the neighborhood from watching.

What brought the fledgling doctor in the first place to a wild and untamed town like Dodge? A few were medical misfits who turned to the West as a field less critical of their talents and background. No one questioned their credentials or explored their past. If they called themselves "doctor," that they were. And accepted as such, they enjoyed, generally at least, the same respect and immunity from violence as the teacher, minister, or judge.

Some, too, were attracted by life in the West and its promise of adventure. Dr. O. H. Simpson's sister had married Walter Chisum of the famous Chisum Ranch. Through this connection Simpson met such frontier characters as Billy the Kid, Pat Garrett, and Bill Hickok, and became familiar with their stories. "So you see," he wrote, "I am steeped in such lore. I just couldn't get away from it—it got into my blood."

On the whole, Dodge City was fortunate. The stalwart handful of doctors who served the community throughout its turbulent years were a gallant band of dedicated men to whom that service was its own reward.

Such a one was Dodge's first physician, Dr. Thomas L. McCarty, who deserves a proud position in the

Southwest's hall of fame. McCarty, born in Indiana
and only twenty-three when he came to Dodge, was
unusual in that he had formally studied medicine at
the Rush Medical College in Philadelphia. He had a
brother-in-law in the Indian Territory south of Dodge
and, seeking a challenge for his talents, headed
West in 1871. The kinsman failed to meet him, but
while waiting, McCarty was infected by the spirit
of rough adventure in the city, and set up an office
in Herman Fringer's drugstore in the center of town.

A descendant of Dodge City pioneers records that
"Dr. McCarty was the only man in the early days
of Dodge to cling to the habits of civilization. He
was an immaculate dresser, wearing broadcloth suits,
stiff white shirt with wing collar and white bow tie,
kid gloves, and shoes instead of boots—not to over-
look the daily shave." Old-timers acknowledged that
it was only McCarty's innate dignity and recognized
humanity that enabled him to violate the frontier
code of dress and manner, and still survive in Dodge
throughout the roaring seventies and eighties.

Frontier life being what it was, with buffalo hunting, Indian fighting, and almost daily gunplay in the
city and on the Plains, a large part of the doctor's
practice was surgery. Pregnant wives whose time
had come would get by on their own with an amateur midwife's assistance, or would have their baby
delivered by the army physician at Fort Dodge, Dr.
William S. Tremaine. Otherwise, women patients

were unwelcome in the frontier doctor's office, if for
no other reason than that the multiple layers of
petticoats, coupled with feminine prudery, made adequate medical examination difficult.

Most of the doctor's patients were Plainsmen and
cowboys injured on the prairie, suffering from knife
cuts, broken bones, Indian arrowheads, and bullet
wounds. Those unable to ride a horse were brought
into Dodge or the nearest community on a travois,
or improvised stretcher. This consisted of two poles
attached to either side of the horse's withers, with a
blanket stretched between them. On this contraption
the victim was dragged to the doctor's office over
many miles of rough terrain, a good test of his
fortitude and chances of survival.

More often than not the doctor was summoned to
the patient—sometimes at gunpoint if he resisted. The
friends of a wounded outlaw might forcibly keep
the doctor at the patient's side until recovery was
complete, or the gunman died, in which latter case
the doctor was threatened with the same fate. For
this reason the physician generally carried a gun,
knowing that in such situations he had a distinct
advantage. He would be first to detect the signs of
approaching death, and could make a break for
freedom before his captors recognized those signs.

However, most of the doctor's calls were more routine in nature, though routine itself was plagued with
hazards. Almost immediately after Dr. McCarty's

arrival in Dodge a cowboy camping outside the city was struck by a freight wagon which badly mangled a foot. Young Tom was obliged to amputate the infected limb, and prepared to do so by the light of two candles held by the victim's friends. With whiskey given as an anesthetic, and also drunk by the attending cowboys to keep the patient company, one of the assistants dropped his candle, forcing the doctor to operate by the light of a single taper held shakily aloft by an intoxicated cowboy.

While chloroform was available as an anesthetic, whiskey was preferred by frontier patients faced with surgery. Known as a certain cure for snakebite, it was equally welcome if an Indian arrowhead or bullet had to be extracted. Moreover, it added a festive, sociable aura to the operation. Friends who insisted on being present at the bedside kept up with the patient, drink for drink, until the doctor finished by treating both patient and well-wishers for inebriation.

Dodge, as noted, had its own version of the Keeley cure for alcoholics. Drunks were thrown into the well on Front Street till they sobered up. But it did not change the frontier belief that liquor was nature's remedy for almost everything. There was, for example, a local cure for baldness, namely: "One quart of clear tar, one quart of whiskey, one quart of honey or molasses. Stir thoroughly, heat briefly, skim off the tar, and drink the remainder." It did not grow hair, but it made a man forget his baldness.

Such ignorance and superstitions were the nemeses of frontier medical practice. When a dose of powder was administered to a housewife suffering from constipation, the husband later refused to let the doctor inspect the patient with a lighted candle. His wife, he explained, was likely to blow up. To the men of Dodge there was only one kind of powder: gunpowder. The husband assumed that the doctor had plied his wife with explosives as a means of blasting out her bowels.

Then there was, of course, the reliance on home remedies. Health almanacs printed and sold by patent-medicine companies were as common in Dodge City as the family Bible, and carried equal weight. Medicine shows that visited the city, peddling Indian nostrums, caused more illnesses than cures. Summoned to attend a dying infant, Dr. Crumbine learned that the child had been given a potion "guaranteed to keep baby from crying." It was a blend of narcotics, alcohol, and sugar.

When a patient died, the doctor was expected to forego his fee, since his services had failed to avert the tragedy. Even with a successful cure, he was often obliged to accept "payment in trade," which meant eggs, butter, ham, and chickens.

Hygiene was given scant consideration in Dodge

City or surrounding dwellings on the Plains. There was no indoor sanitation and no insulation against windblown dirt and insects. Dr. Crumbine, whose house calls covered an area within a radius of fifty miles from Dodge, found one hut he visited so badly infested with ticks and bedbugs that, on leaving, "everything I had on or with me had to be discarded, cast to the wide open spaces on my way home."

There were of course no telephones by which to summon the doctor in a crisis. The Plains people around Dodge invented their own grapevine for communication. A sheet hung from a rooftop or a second-story window, with a lantern substituted for the sheet at night, signaled a distant neighbor that a resident was ill. The neighbor, by like devices, relayed that message to the next home down the line; and so on from house to house until the call for help reached Dodge. At that point and at any hour of the day or night the doctor saddled his horse and set out across the Plains.

With him, besides his surgical case and Colt revolver, went other emergency equipment: a spade, a carpenter's saw, a lantern, a hammer, and a wire cutter—by which to dig the buggy free of miring sand, repair a wheel, or cut a fence. Much of the doctor's exertions went to reaching the bedside of his patient. Wrote Dr. Arthur Hertzler regarding his frontier practice, "By far the greater part of it was hitch up, plug along the roads, make a call, plug back again at the same old weary pace. Get stuck in the mud, get out somehow, meet a snowdrift, shovel out or cut the fence and drive around the snowdrift."

Many were the nights that the doctor's buggy was his only couch. As a result he was often riddled by the fever of a cold, feeling closer to death than some of his hypochondriacal patients. Alone on the Plains he relied on his rifle for both protection and relief from boredom, taking pot shots at jackrabbits, prairie dogs, and owls. If no game was around he practiced his marksmanship on fence posts. Recorded Dr. Hertzler in his memoirs, "I have fired as many as five hundred rounds on a single trip."

Doctors in Dodge, and in other cowtowns, were obliged to perform assorted services outside their immediate profession. Tom McCarty became town coroner, an important office since so many deaths by violence called for investigation. Also, there being no veterinarians in Dodge, the local physicians were called upon to treat sick and injured animals, an ill horse being of as much concern as an ailing wife or child. A prize pony saved by medical skill was a cause for lasting gratitude. Countless colts were named after Dr. Crumbine, until the doctor got used to seeing, in the sports pages of Kansas City journals, such headlines as "Dr. Crumbine snatches purse at track!"

Until doctors McCarty and Crumbine landed in Dodge, dentistry was practiced by the local smithy using a twopenny nail, a hammer, and a pair of pliers for extractions. But the newly arrived doctors shortly found themselves expected to cure aching teeth. With no X ray to pinpoint the trouble, it was up to the patient to identify the offending cuspid— a process that left considerable room for error.

Crumbine recalls yanking an irritable cowboy's tooth, only to find that he had pulled the wrong one, and the aching tooth remained. Quickly aware of the mistake, the cowboy flashed his gun and demanded that the tooth be put back. "I never had done such a thing," admitted Crumbine, "but I put it back in its socket, whacked it with a mallet, and so help me, it stayed put!" The good doctor modestly added: "It had only a single root."

Unlike Dr. Tom McCarty, whose eastern dress and manners were discounted by his popularity, a newly arrived physician did well to conform to the customs and attire of his likely clientele. When Oscar H. Simpson, later known as the "Dude Dentist of Dodge City," first reached town, he ignored the advice of Sam Galland, proprietor of the Great Western Hotel, where Simpson stopped. He appeared on the street in a cutaway coat, pinstripe trousers, and (abomination of abominations) high silk topper!

When he entered the Long Branch and asked for

milk, the provocation was complete. Declaring "he ain't weaned yet!" the customers rushed Simpson out into the street, drew their guns, and made a target of the high silk hat, while Simpson made a target of the nearest shelter. His next appearance in public was in wide-brimmed cowboy hat, embroidered vest, and high-heeled boots, which became his professional attire in the office.

Doc Holliday made no such error. He had made the rounds from Dallas to Wichita and established his reputation as gunfighter, gambler, and a man of far more skills than dentistry. When he arrived in Dodge in the spring of 1878 he looked for the best hotel in town, checked in at the Dodge House, and decked himself out in conventional frontier attire, not forgetting his six-gun in its shoulder holster. Out on the street he entered the Long Branch, and demanded whiskey—straight.

Beside Doc at the bar was a short, intelligent-looking character in the starched shirt, black string tie, and cutaway that were the trademark of the professional gambler. They introduced themselves, the stranger declaring his name to be Luke Short. Luke announced that a poker game was brewing in a back room and asked if the newcomer cared to join them. Doc nodded. A poker game may not have been the orthodox way to establish oneself as a doctor or dentist in the city, but it was by far the quickest and most effective. Three days later, in the Dodge City *Times*, appeared the announcement:

J. H. Holliday, Dentist, very respectfully offers his professional services to the citizens of Dodge City and surrounding country during the summer. Office at room No. 24, Dodge House. Where satisfaction is not given, money will be refunded.

Holliday, according to Heinie Schmidt, did a thriving business. Whether or not he ever refunded a patient's money for unsatisfactory performance, he did pay for one professional mistake. The patient involved was none other than Clay Allison, the Texas gunman who had tried all day to ease an aching tooth with too much whiskey. On entering Doc's office Allison fired several shots through the ceiling to establish his identity as one not to be trifled with.

Doc once told a friend that "the only time he wasn't nervous was when he was in a fight or working on someone's teeth." But that morning seems to have marked an exception. A handy man with a gun himself, Holliday was no match for Allison; and the Texan was in an ugly mood.

Whatever the cause, Holliday made the common error which Dr. Crumbine had succumbed to: he pulled the wrong tooth. Clay's fury was instant and implacable. According to Heinie Schmidt's report, based no doubt on hearsay, "Allison made Holliday lie down in the chair, and either pulled or knocked out one of his teeth in return. I am informed on reliable authority that Holliday never had this tooth replaced." Not long after, Doc was on his way to Tombstone, preferring the hazards of a frontier mining camp to those of cowtown dentistry.

Other Dodge City doctors, however, remained faithful to their posts, many making major contributions to frontier society and medicine in general. Tom McCarty, who practiced medicine in Dodge for fifty-eight years, became, according to Lola A. Harper, "the oldest and best known surgeon and physician in the West." In addition to his medical practice, he served as school superintendent, donated the site for the first church, and promoted many recreational facilities in Dodge. His son, Claude, was the first child born in the city and successfully followed in his father's footsteps. Together, father and son established the only early hospital in Dodge. Claude also became a pioneer in radiological research and perfected one of the first X-ray machines.

Samuel Crumbine did more perhaps than any other to promote the construction of sanitary facilities in Dodge, and achieved a statewide reputation in the field of hygiene. Dr. Charles A. Milton, whose quiet, self-effacing manner gained him little publicity, was a diligent worker for progressive government in the city. O. H. Simpson, in turn, introduced a new wrinkle in frontier practice. On the back of a buckboard he rigged up a dental office with his cases of equipment strapped behind. Touring the cowtowns with this mobile office, he extended his services to most of southwest Kansas.

Simpson finished his days in Dodge with a surprising shift of occupation, switching from dentist to accomplished sculptor. Besides the graveyard markers he designed, two of his works are still displayed on Boot Hill: the carved heads of a pair of Longhorns, commemorating Dodge's great days as a cattle town, and, with similar purpose, the life-size statue of a cowboy of the Plains. On a plaque affixed to the statue are the simple words:

On the Ashes of My Campfire This City is Built.

12

Horse Thieves, Outlaws, and Cattle Rustlers

> Now they picked a limb that looked the best
> On the tallest tree that stood on that crest;
> With a lariat rope they hanged that pest,
> For such was the code of the great Southwest.
> *Texas Trail to Dodge City*

To the booted, six-gun citizens of Dodge, two items were more precious than all the gold and silver in Virginia City. One was the cowboy's horse, and the other was his saddle.

The saddle, on which he spent a large part of his life as well as a large part of his wages, was a highly personal possession. It was often custom made or altered to his needs and whims. His own weight and riding habits helped to shape its contours, till it fitted his posterior like a glove. He might wager his gun, his shirt, and even his horse, in a poker game but never his saddle.

The saddle had another hidden asset. It was not

likely to be stolen, except by one in desperate need. Being personally conditioned by its owner, it was not apt to suit another. By the same token, it could not be readily sold by the thief, since, like a well-worn pair of shoes, it was comfortable only to its owner.

But a man's horse was a different matter. It could readily be disposed of in the open market, or be used by the thief himself for transportation and flight. The Plains Indians were eager purchasers of stolen horses, besides being competent horse thieves in their own right. Fort Dodge was plagued by Indian thefts of army mules and horses, with the Comanches being the prime offenders. The more successful among them sometimes owned a string of from fifty to a hundred stolen animals. Wrote Colonel Dodge, commanding the fort:

> Where all are such magnificent thieves, it is difficult to decide which of the Plains tribes deserves the palm for stealing. The Indians themselves give it to the Comanches . . . who for crawling into a camp, cutting hobbles and lariat ropes, and getting off with animals undiscovered, are unsurpassed. . . . I have known a Comanche to crawl into a bivouac where a dozen men were sleeping, each with his horse tied to his wrist by the lariat, cut a rope within six feet of a sleeper's person, and get off with the horse without waking a soul.

A cowboy or hunter without a horse was helpless on the prairie. The horse was essential to his trade, and often to his very life. As a result the horse thief was the lowest form of criminal, demanding quick chastisement without benefit of trial. In Dodge City today, on Boot Hill, stands a gnarled buttonwood with a noosed rope about one branch and a plaque that reads "The Hanging Tree"—a theatrical prop reminding the viewer that "such was the code of the great Southwest."

Actually, there were no recorded lynchings in Dodge City, though numerous thefts took place both in and around the town. After the 1873 depression, which left many railroad crews and other laborers out of work, horse stealing was both a profitable and an exciting way of life. Throughout the seventies, a wave of such robberies swept Kansas, with Dodge City suffering the lion's share. A bulletin from Fort Dodge announced: "Horse thieving is a little too bold and frequent to be longer endured without more stringent measures than a short term in the penitentiary. Some of these bold operators will some fine evening be taken in the most approved and summary style."

In 1878 the Dodge City *Times* reported, "Horse stealing has taken a fresh start in the country. . . . The officers of Ford County are on the alert and watch with a vigilant eye every suspicious character lurking in our midst." A newspaper correspondent in Dodge declared: "The Arkansas valley is infested by a bold gang of horse-thieves. A vigilance committee has been organized at Dodge City, and it would not be surprising if some of the telegraph poles were found ornamented some of these days."

There were indeed frequent summary hangings on the Plains beyond the watchful eyes of lawmen. When two leaders of a gang of horse thieves were suspended from a tree above a blazing fire and thus burned to death, the Dodge City *Globe* deplored the "barbaric act." Under County Sheriff Masterson, horse thieves were properly brought to trial—and frequently acquitted by juries unwilling to incur their wrath. The fact was that horse owners were more anxious to regain their prize animals than to see the culprits punished, and a thief could often sell stolen horses back to the original owner, with no questions asked.

However, things did not always work out to the thief's convenience or immunity. Twelve miles northeast of Dodge was Horse Thief Canyon, a fifty-foot gully—deep for the Plains—which provided a hangout and refuge for rustlers. But this hideout, once discovered, became the horse thief's nemesis. Since lynchings were frowned on in Dodge, irate victims of the rustlers could bring their captured predators to the canyon for execution beyond the reach or knowledge of the law; the last hanging took place there in 1885.

One of Dodge City's more colorful characters was a half-breed Mexican rustler named Benjamin F.

Hodges. Ben had limped into town in 1876 with both heels hamstrung by vigilantes for stealing horses. Perhaps because of his affliction, perhaps because of the outrageous but amusing lies he told about his kinship with Mexican aristocracy, the locals took pity on Ben. He shuffled about on his maimed feet, cadging drinks and generally living off the town. Later, when Dodge had been thoroughly tamed, Ben was to wear a marshal's badge, thus somewhat redeeming his misspent life, but too crippled to be of effective service.

Unlike the professional gunman or bounty hunter —lone operators by the nature of their trade—horse thieves and cattle rustlers, as well as highwaymen and railroad bandits, worked generally in gangs under the leadership of one or more daring individuals who planned and supervised their operations. Outstanding among these ringleaders was Dutch Henry, christened by one Dodge City chronicler the "Rob Roy of the Plains." Shy of identity, outlaws were inclined to travel under what was referred to as "road names." No one was certain what Dutch Henry's surname was, but many believed it to be Born or Borne.

Dutch Henry was described as "a genteel-looking fellow to have been a horse thief. Dressed in his usual white linen shirt and well-cut suit, he could have passed for a professional man of German descent. He had black hair and a mustache, a long face and Roman nose. His black eyes were bright and penetrating, denoting considerable intelligence."

Despite this respectable appearance, his name was anathema in Dodge. The local newspaper warned of Dutch Henry's rumored presence in the neighborhood as a service to its readers. (The *Globe*, August 6, 1878: "Dutch Henry is again on his own stamping ground south of Dodge.") Such announcements prompted ranchers to stand guard over their livestock through the night, armed and ready to fight off Henry and his gang.

Little was known about Dutch's past, except that he had been a trooper under General Custer, and later been caught and jailed for running off with a string of army mules. He escaped from jail, and took to the Plains to become the leading horse thief on the frontier—a reputation he modestly disclaimed. In time he commanded an army of three hundred horse thieves, with associated bands in other areas of the Southwest, all operating as a mighty frontier underworld. Wrote one Western chronicler:

> Henry's fame as a horse-thief extended far and wide. Many tales of reckless daring were told about him; how handy he was with a revolver; his powerful influence over his confederates; how he rode his magnificent sorrel horse at the head of his band with the dignity of a general; how desperately he fought when pursued; and how he always escaped his captors.

Wyatt Earp, the most famous of Dodge City marshals, became the prototype of the typical Western lawman. *The Kansas State Historical Society, Topeka*

William B. "Bat" Masterson, a popular lawman during Dodge City's turbulent years. *The Kansas State Historical Society, Topeka*

Bill Tilghman, the upright peace officer of Dodge, was later shot by a United States agent in Oklahoma. *The University of Oklahoma, Norman*

Mysterious Dave Mather—gambler, onetime marshal, and saloon proprietor. *W. S. Campbell Collection, Western History Collections, University of Oklahoma Library*

The famous Colt forty-five "peacemaker" was exactly what its name implied, in the hands of Dodge City's equally famous lawmen. *W. S. Campbell Collection, Western History Collections, University of Oklahoma Library*

Chief Santanta of the Kiowas, the leader of Indian raids in the vicinity of Dodge, preferred death to capture. *Smithsonian Institution*

Chalkley M. Beeson, musician and cattleman, owned the COD Ranch outside of Dodge. *The Kansas State Historical Society, Topeka*

In addition to tables for gambling and drinking, Dodge City dance
halls often provided stage entertainment. *Frank Leslie's Illustrated
Newspaper*

This shady lady of Dodge City dance halls was known only as Squirrel Tooth Alice. *Cultural Heritage and Arts Society*

Eddie Foy, a popular performer in Dodge City dance halls. *New York Public Library Photo Collection*

Ben Thompson, called "the most dangerous killer in the West," terrorized Wichita before moving on to Dodge. He later became a Texas marshal. *Rose Collection, Western Historical Collections, University of Oklahoma Library*

Clay Allison, at the age of twenty-six, was one of the many famous gunmen who challenged Marshal Wyatt Earp's control of Dodge. *Rose Collection, Western Historical Collections, University of Oklahoma Library*

A general view of Fort Dodge about 1879, from the high ground looking south toward the Arkansas River. *Fort Dodge Historical Society*

John "Doc" Holliday—gunfighter, gambler, and Dodge City dentist—was doomed by tuberculosis. *The Kansas State Historical Society, Topeka*

The bar at the Long Branch Saloon was the epitome of elegance, and a favorite rendezvous throughout Dodge City's thirsty years.
The Kansas State Historical Society, Topeka

The City Drug Store was Dodge's "medical center" in the early days. In this photo the veteran doctor Thomas L. McCarty is shown (light-colored trousers) in the foreground. *The Kansas State Historical Society, Topeka*

The Dodge City Cowboy Band, organized by Chalkley Beeson, as it appeared in 1886. *The Kansas State Historical Society, Topeka*

A. B. Webster, Dodge's "reform" mayor and proprietor of the Alamo, was a feature figure in the city's great saloon war. *W. S. Campbell Collection, Western History Collections, University of Oklahoma Library*

The two-story Dodge House, George B. Cox, proprietor, was the city's leading hostelry for two decades. *The Kansas State Historical Society, Topeka*

Larry Deger was marshal of Dodge City in 1876–77, and was later elected mayor. *Fort Dodge Historical Society*

Dodge City's "peace commission," 1883. Standing (left to right):
William H. Harris, Luke Short, Bat Masterson, W. F. Petillon.
Seated (left to right): Charles Bassett, Wyatt Earp, Frank Mc-
Clean, Neal Brown. *The Kansas State Historical Society, Topeka*

The Great Blizzard of 1886 buried the trains that crossed the prairies and dealt a death blow to the cattle trade. *Fort Dodge Historical Society*

Dr. O. H. Simpson's statue of the typical Dodge City cowboy still stands on Boot Hill. *W. S. Campbell Collection, Western History Collections, University of Oklahoma Library*

His flights from custody were as bizarre as the rest of his career. "He makes his escape through the key-holes of jail doors," the *Globe* reported with a sly dig at his jailers. Trapped on the prairie by two armed officers when he happened to be without his guns, Henry so confused his captors that one of them drew his revolver and shot the other by mistake, thus allowing Henry to escape across the Plains unharmed. He appeared so unassailable that ranchers with suddenly empty corrals would send word to Henry to keep an eye out for the stolen horses, knowing, since Henry had doubtless stolen them himself, that the animals would be returned for the reward.

Dutch was finally cornered in the small town of Trinidad across the Kansas-Colorado border as he was bent over a pool table trying to sink the number three ball in a corner pocket. Since he was wanted in Dodge, Bat Masterson rode in to claim him. But Dutch was now something of a property. The Colorado authorities were reluctant to release him, hoping to hear of a price upon his head. Bat, however, badly wanted the man he had pursued for countless months; he paid five hundred dollars for the privilege of bringing Henry back to Dodge. Just where that money came from is not clear—conceivably from Bat's own pocket.

It was in Dodge City's jail that Dutch suffered the narrowest escape of his career. He had so many enemies by now, so many who had suffered losses at his hands, that an attempt upon his life was not surprising. That night, person or persons unknown crept up to the window of the jail and repeatedly fired through the bars at Dutch as he lay sleeping on a cot. But Henry was one who bore a charmed life; none of the bullets found its mark. The next day he was tried and acquitted "for lack of sufficient evidence." He took to the Plains again to continue his episodic career like the hero of a weekly television series.

Cattle rustling, though less of a crime than horse stealing, was a common offense in the neighborhood of Dodge once the Texas Longhorns started coming to that city. In the case of stray, unbranded steers called "mavericks"—named after Texas ranchman Samuel Maverick, who was disinclined to brand his cattle—it was simply a matter of rounding them up and appropriating them. When it came to branded Longhorns coming up the Texas trails, these could be weeded out of a sleeping herd at night, or could be gathered up as the cattle were scattered by a deliberately induced stampede.

Then came the matter of changing the brands as one might change the license on a stolen car. Most rustlers used a "running iron" which differed from the stamping iron (heated and pressed into the hide to leave its mark) in that it was pointed and used as a pencil to doctor a registered brand. With this red-hot iron, for example, a "C" could easily be closed to make an "O," or a "3" could be changed to an "8" or "B." A man who was caught with a running iron on the Plains was automatically regarded as a rustler. He was either shot or hanged on the spot, or turned over to the county sheriff.

Operating around Dodge City and eventually expanding his activities to much of southern Kansas was twenty-three-year-old Dave Rudabaugh, whom Wyatt Earp called "about the most notorious outlaw in the range country; rustler and robber by trade with the added specialty of killing jailers in the breaks for liberty at which he was invariably successful whenever he was arrested." Yes, he was versatile, shifting from highway robbery and cattle rustling to hijacking railroad trains as opportunity occurred.

Earp was one of the first peace officers to track down Rudabaugh, pursuing him into Texas only to learn from Doc Holliday, whom he first met at Fort Griffin, that the bandit had doubled back on his tracks and was heading into Kansas. Here Wyatt lost the trail, and Sheriff Bat Masterson of Dodge took up the pursuit. What Bat didn't know, but later learned, was that Rudabaugh and his partner Mike Roarke had concocted a scheme to hijack one of the westbound Santa Fe express trains.

The Great Train Robbery, as Dodge newsmen liked to call it, was actually more comedy than drama. The six bandits, with faces blackened for disguise, assembled at a water tank some miles west of Dodge, where they counted on the locomotive stopping. But the engineer had taken on sufficient water earlier and, waving genially to the dirty-faced hoboes, sped on past them. The disgruntled bandits repaired to the tiny nearby depot of Kinsey, where Andrew Kinkade, the young station master, bravely refused to open the safe, insisting he didn't have the key.

The bandits contemplated blowing out Kinkade's brains, when the whistle of a second westbound train was heard. The gang ignored Kinkade and raced to the platform, while the stationmaster raced across the tracks, putting the train between him and the bandits, and shouted to the locomotive engineer, "Look out! Six armed men on the platform!"

The warning came too late. Two of Rudabaugh's gang mounted the locomotive to capture the engineer at gunpoint. Two others started through the train to rob the passengers. The third pair tried to board the freight car, where they pointed their rifles at expressman Harry A. Brown and demanded the cargo. Brown calmly reached for his six-gun, and, while a half dozen bullets were fired at him, shot one of the bandits in the face and forced the other to retreat.

Hearing the shooting, the two captors of the engineer leaped from the locomotive to come to the aid of their comrades in the rear. Whereupon the engineer started up the train, leaving them stranded. The two bandits holding up the passengers, alarmed at finding the train moving with their comrades being left behind, leaped off the cars without having collected their anticipated loot. For the Rudabaugh-Roarke gang the attempted robbery was a sensational fiasco.

The Santa Fe Railroad offered a reward for capture of the gang. Bat Masterson organized a posse that included Deputy Sheriff John Joshua Webb, Kinch Riley, a companion of Bat's in the Battle of Adobe Walls, and Prairie Dog Dave Morrow. They located the robbers camped several miles outside of Dodge. Webb, who was unknown to the gang, approached the camp posing as a horse thief and offered to lead them to an accessible corral where they could take their pick of valuable horses. The bandits fell for the ruse, and were led directly into the hands of Masterson and the awaiting posse.

While Rudabaugh and one of his men were captured, Mike Roarke and four others escaped the trap. Bat led his prisoners back to Dodge, while a second posse under Jim Masterson and Charlie Bassett pursued Roarke and his men as far as Indian Territory, which the lawmen lacked authority to enter. It seemed as if Roarke was home free, but one of his men later put the finger on him when he was back in circulation, and Roarke was nabbed and sentenced to ten years in the penitentiary.

There was a curious sequel to this affair which illustrates how often the lawman discarded his badge to become the renegade. Two years later, in 1880, John Webb was serving in Las Vegas, New Mexico, as city marshal. In a personal quarrel he shot and killed a man and was arrested, tried, and sentenced to be hanged. He sought to escape the sentence by breaking jail. The person reported to have engineered the murderer's planned escape was none other than Dave Rudabaugh, the man that Webb had helped Bat Masterson capture.

Often the outlaws were cowboys who had simply "gone wrong"—temporarily down on their luck and turning to robbery as an expedient. Such was Sam Bass, regarded by his companions as "a hail-fellow-well-met, never vicious, true to his friends, and generous with his money." In the Robin Hood tradition he was so popular for half a century that someone wrote a poem about him, which has helped to keep his name alive. It seems that in 1876, Sam and a pal named Joel Collins were hired to bring a herd of Texas cattle up to Dodge, where they sold them for eight thousand dollars. That deal was their undoing.

The money, of course, belonged to the owner of the herd. But the temptations of Dodge City were too much for Sam and Joel. In a night of celebration they drank and gambled until so much of their money was gone that they did not dare return to Texas.

To recoup what they had lost they turned to robbery. Joel Collins, the brains of the partnership, recruited some footloose souls in Dodge and formed the Collins gang. Holding up stagecoaches proved to be small pickings, and they turned to hijacking railroad trains. One haul netted them sixty thousand dollars, after which the gang split up. Sam Bass and a man named Davis headed back for Texas, crossing Kansas in a horse and buggy and posing as footloose cowboys looking for a homestead.

Not far from Dodge they holed up near a creek, where they were discovered by a band of soldiers hunting for them. The bluecoats were unaware of their identity. They invited the innocent-looking bandits to share their camp for the night and enjoy their rations. Sam and Davis entertained their hosts with colorful tales of the "Sam Bass-Collins gang," including details of their robberies. The next morning they parted company, and the unsuspecting soldiers wished them well in their expedition.

Ironically, it was not until Sam Bass got back to Texas, certain he was home free, that a group of Texas Rangers recognized him from his pictures in the Kansas papers. Sam was captured in a bloody skirmish that left the bandit mortally wounded. Though aware he was dying he stuck to the outlaw's code of silence.

"I ain't talkin'," he told his captors. "It's against

my profession. If a man knows anything, he ought to die with it. I'm goin' to hell anyhow."

The anonymous author of the *Ballad of Sam Bass* apparently agreed with Sam. The last two lines of his epic read:

Perhaps he's gone to heaven, there's none of us can say,
But if I'm right in my surmise, he's gone the other way.

13

High Jinks on the Plaza

> Come, all soft-hearted tenderfeet,
>   If you want to have some fun;
> Go live among the cowboys,
>   They'll show you how it's done.
> *Cowboy Songs and Frontier Ballads*

High spirits and low humor were common to the frontier. They were cultivated and forgiven in an age and a society which offered no canned entertainment such as radio, movies, television, and recorded music.

True, Dodge had its dance halls, its Comique Theater and Lady Gay Varieties, and the custom of lassoing chorus girls from the ringside seats was considered part of the entertainment. But in general the stage shows were too tame for the irrepressible cowboys, who often invented their own bizarre amusements—with the wide, convenient Plaza between the

the North and South Sides serving as an amphitheater.

Robert M. Wright, a central figure if not the leading citizen of Dodge, remarked, "Her code of morals is the honor of thieves, and decency she knows not." But he added the redeeming comment: "She is a merry town and the only visible support of a great many of her citizens is jocularity." Perhaps the harshness of frontier life demanded some comic relief. As another old-timer put it, "Dodge's sense of humor was exaggerated and worked overtime."

Often all that was needed for diversion, along with a certain amount of inventiveness, was an out-of-town greenhorn, preferably from the East, to serve as scapegoat. In fact, baiting the innocent tenderfoot was a favorite form of entertainment. When Elias Cohn, a clothing salesman, visited the city, he made the mistake of boasting about the Indians he had encountered in his travels and his bravery in battling the redskins.

This gave birth to Dodge's famous "Indian Act." While one group of citizens invited the drummer to join them in a hunting expedition on the Plains, another group organized by Mayor Kelley donned Indian buckskins, headdress, and war paint, and galloped out to intercept the hunters.

Dodge citizens climbed to their roofs or shinnied up telegraph poles to view the fun as, on signal, the whooping "Comanches" rose from their ambush and descended on the hunting party. "Indians! Run for your life!" shouted Kelley. Elias Cohn needed no such prompting. With one look at the charging warriors, he whirled his horse around and "rode the wind" toward Dodge, losing his deerstalker's cap in flight.

The bedeviled Cohn was convinced his end had come as the savages pressed hard upon his heels. But as the victim and his pursuers galloped into town to be hilariously greeted by its citizens, Elias realized he'd been taken. Drinks all around at the Long Branch were in order, with Cohn footing the bill to atone for his gullibility. Kidded about the loss of his hat, Elias insisted it had blown off. "No," Mayor Kelley told him, "it was pushed off when your hair stood on end."

The Indian Act was performed successfully on many a dude and tenderfoot. But it backfired in the case of one shrewd drummer named Hank Harris. Invited to join the proverbial hunting expedition, and provided with a shotgun loaded with blanks, Harris suspected a trick. He secreted his own revolver in his belt, loaded with live ammunition. When the masquerading Indians charged the party and saloonkeeper P. L. Beatty shouted, "Run for your life!" Harris not only stood his ground, but drew his revolver and fired at the "tribal chief." The attacking horde vanished like chaff before the wind.

That evening, drinks at the Long Branch were on the "Indians."

Drunks were a favorite butt of jokes, with results that often cured the subject of his taste for alcohol. An inebriated lawyer made a habitual nuisance of himself at the Alhambra, and once too often passed out on the floor. Local wags carried him out to the street, dressed him in a funeral shroud, powdered his face to simulate the pallor of death, and laid him in a pine coffin. A wreath of sunflowers was placed on his chest, with lighted candles at his head and feet.

When the victim came shakily to his senses and read his own epitaph, "Gone but we don't know where," he struggled from the coffin, staggered into the saloon, and peered at his haggard features in the mirror behind the bar. Too thoroughly shaken even to request a reassuring drink, he reportedly swore off alcohol for good.

Dr. Sam Crumbine, boarding at the Dodge House, was awakened one morning by raucous laughter from the Plaza. Rushing to the window, he was greeted by a farcical sight. A nearly hysterical town drunk in his nightshirt was being pursued by a seemingly avaricious bear. Later Crumbine learned that the drunk had been put to bed by kindly citizens, who then conceived of a cure for his addiction.

An organ grinder was visiting town accompanied by a dancing bear. The Good Samaritans who had put the drunk to bed had hired the bear, poured honey over the sleeping victim, and turned the animal loose to enjoy the honey. When the boozy sleeper awoke to find a bear on top of him, licking his chops with obvious relish, he threw off the covers and fled to the street, with the bear in hot pursuit. As both headed out of town the organ grinder, fearful of losing his mascot, joined the chase. The bear was caught and the terrified drunk was returned to bed to consider the wages of intemperance.

Dodge had its own version of the hotfoot in the form of a specially concocted liniment named Hokey Pokey. Hokey Pokey was vaunted to the greenhorn as a cure for everything from baldness to aching feet—a secret formula invented by the Indians. Actually it was a potent mixture of alcohol, powdered Mexican peppers, and other strong irritants. Applied to the bald pate of an innocent cowboy anxious to grow hair, or the sore feet of a greenhorn returning from a hunting expedition, it caused a violent burning sensation that sent the victim diving into the nearest water barrel.

Since the average cowboy regarded himself as something of a Romeo, the more obnoxious self-styled lady killers were sometimes bombarded with letters from out-of-town females proposing marriage. If the victim succumbed to any of these phony offers, an ancient Indian squaw was hired to appear at the

depot on the day assigned, to claim her future husband. When the horrified groom attempted to re-
nege, the town sided with the squaw—and a shotgun marriage was staged on the Plaza with a local
townsman posing as the minister. Only after the de-
jected groom, convinced he was chained for life to
a harridan half-breed, repented of his wolfish ways,
was he told of being the dupe of his own arrogance.

The kingpin of pranksters in Dodge City was a
mythical character named "Luke McGlue." Luke
took the blame for tricks that either went awry or
exceeded the limits of the law. He came into existence when a drummer peddling choice cigars arrived in town and tethered his team on Front Street
while he entered the Alhambra for a drink. In his
absence, the loitering cowboys did what came naturally: they peered into his wagon and helped themselves to the cigars.

Soon every idler on the street, perched contentedly on steps or railing, was openly relishing a
choice Havana. When the drummer emerged from
the saloon and saw the empty wagon and the puffing
cowboys, he reported the theft to Wyatt Earp. The
marshal asked the first smoker that he approached
where he had gotten the cigar. "Luke McGlue gave
it to me," said the cowboy, improvising.

Picking up the cue, his neighbor gave the same response. And all down the line the ready answer was,
"I got it from Luke McGlue." But Luke, the myste-

rious benefactor, could not be found; and those who acknowledged his generosity could not be held to blame. Thereafter the light-fingered Luke McGlue, Dodge City's nonexistent Robin Hood, was often reported by the local papers as being involved in various mischievous misdemeanors that baffled the authorities.

When the Santa Fe Trail was being widened the graders unearthed a human skull, probably that of a buffalo hunter, with an Indian arrowhead embedded in its base. It was put on public display as a curiosity, and an obnoxious wag attempted to demonstrate his wit by engaging the skull in daily conversation.

"Say, old-timer," he would crack, "can I get you something for that headache?"

His audience tired of this dialogue and saw its chance when a touring ventriloquist arrived in town. The performer was hired to stand by; and when the jolly interlocutor went into his act, the ventriloquist threw his voice into the wide mouthpiece of the skull.

"You can make fun of these bones of mine," the skull said. "But my spirit ain't dead and it'll be around tonight to h-a-a-nt you!"

The badly shaken joker hurried into the Alhambra for a badly needed drink, and his conversations with the skull were discontinued.

An uninitiated Easterner appearing on the streets

of Dodge in fancy clothes was the butt of more than
verbal jests. Top hats were legitimate targets for a
six-gun; and affected mannerisms or too-elegant attire might lead to a ducking in one of the water-
filled barrels that lined the wooden sidewalks. When
Eddie Foy arrived in town for an engagement at the
Lady Gay, he laid himself wide open for a bit of
hazing.

Wrote Bob Wright regarding Foy's appearance,
"He dressed pretty loud and had a kind of Fifth
Avenue swaggering strut, and made some distaste-
ful jokes about the cowboys." Foy was finally seized
and bound and a hangman's noose was slipped
around his neck. The rope was then tossed over the
crossbar of a telegraph pole and a crowd assembled
for the hanging. Asked if he had any last words before he went to meet his Maker, Eddie had a ready
answer.

"Lots of 'em," he said. "But I could say 'em better
over a bar, if you all would join me at the Long
Branch for my last chance to buy the drinks."

While the proposal didn't save Eddie's life, which
was never in serious danger, it did save his reputation and made him one of the more popular entertainers to appear in Dodge.

In addition to these impromptu high jinks were
the more conventional forms of frontier competition
and amusement. Horses were highly prized among
God's creatures, and flat racing on the Plaza was a

popular sport. High stakes were raised and high
wagers placed, and the animals themselves would
have shamed many an Eastern two-year-old. The
Plains pony was a born competitor. Trained to exhibit
uncanny spurts of speed, essential on the prairie in
hunting antelope or rounding up a stray steer, it was
adapted principally to races of a quarter of a mile.
Hence the term "quarterhorse," still used today.

Billy Tilghman was a leading trainer and breeder
in Dodge. In later years, his gelding named Chant
won the Kentucky Derby. But Bill's favorite horse,
Chief, came to him circuitously. Owned by a Kiowa
chief, it was stolen from the Indian by Dutch Henry,
and later sold by Dutch to Tilghman for eighty-five
dollars. When Chief proved to be a money-maker,
Dutch regretted the sale and demanded the horse
back, threatening to steal him again if Bill refused.

"You steal that horse again, and I'll shoot you,"
Tilghman warned Dutch. Henry considered the matter, and decided, "By Gott, Bill, if you care enough
for that damned horse to shoot me for him, then you
keep him."

Dog racing, too, was popular. Jim "Dog" Kelley
got his nickname from the fine string of thorough-
bred greyhounds and wolfhounds that he kept in
Dodge. Some had been whelped by General Custer's
pack when Kelley had served with Custer and cared
for the officer's hounds. Since the mechanical rabbit
had not been invented as a lure, the dogs were pitted

against the antelope that roamed the surrounding prairies, and the winning dog was the one who, after races of six miles or more, brought down the largest number of the nimble quarry. In one of these contests involving his two prize greyhounds, Kelley collected a record twenty-thousand-dollar stake.

There were no team sports such as those observed in the East, except for a baseball game held between the soldiers of the Fort and Dodge's Fire Hose Company Nine. When the Fort Dodge Clippers lost to the local club by a six-run margin, the soldiers protested bitterly that the Dodge players had been drunk throughout the game. Just how that enabled the city to win was not explained.

Almost any kind of physical combat was spontaneously staged. In May 1877 the Dodge City *Times* reported the results of "an exhibition of the African game of lap-jacket in front of Schulz's harness shop, in which two blacks fought with bull whips for a prize of half-a-dollar." A month later a sixty-five-round prizefight took place in front of the Saratoga Saloon at 4:30 A.M. (a time when no ladies would be present) between two bare-knuckle champions, Nelson Whitman and Red Hanley. Of this event, the *Times* recorded:

> The only injuries sustained by the loser were two ears chewed off, one eye busted and the other disabled, right cheek bone caved in, bridge of the nose broken, seven teeth knocked out, one jaw bone

mashed, one side of the tongue bit off, and several other unimportant fractures and bruises.

Apparently both fighters remained standing to the end, since the reporter added:

Red retired from the ring in disgust.

Target practice in the frontier towns was not so much a sport as a dedication, since a man's life might depend on the sureness of his aim. It was almost by reflex that the gun-toting cowboy shot at doorknobs, bottles, signs, and any convenient target challenging his skill. Competitive claims of prowess led to sometimes orderly contests. According to Marshal Earp, "shooting matches for prestige and money-stakes were daily events."

Not all these shooting matches ended as innocently as they started. Onetime gunman Ed Prather, now running a saloon in Dodge, conceived of a stunt that might attract customers to his establishment. He enlisted the support of another gunslinger named Grant Wells, now an assistant city marshal, in putting on the show. Prather placed a can on top of his head and invited Wells to shoot it off. The marshal did. Wells then borrowed a high silk hat from someone in the audience, set it on his head, and shouted: "Ed, put a hole through this hard-boiled Katy!"

Prather sent a bullet neatly through the crown. "Want to see me put another through the same hole?" he demanded of the crowd. When they expressed some skepticism of his chances, Ed raised his forty-five again and fired. The bullet hit Wells squarely in the forehead, killing him instantly. Prather didn't wait for the applause. He was on his horse and half-way out of town before his audience was sure of what had happened.

Though parades were generally confined to the Fourth of July, when the liberal discharge of fire-crackers, guns, and rifles was approved, Chalkley Beeson's Cowboy Band became a city institution. Organized by the musically talented Beeson in the early 1880s it numbered from eighteen to twenty drums and trumpet players decked in cowboy finery, all with six-guns at their hips with which to punctuate a chord or phrase as their musical whims suggested.

There were, as well, itinerant musicians and traveling bands from out of town that sometimes led to complications on the Plaza, where the tame bull or bulls, pets sacred to the memory of the buffalo, were free to roam. As the Dodge City *Globe* reported:

> The buffalo that runs about town is accustomed to the music of the Cowboy Band. The group is Western in appearance and does not interfere with the peace and happiness of the buffalo. But there are some things the buffalo won't stand. Among them is a strange lot of men blowing horns and marching through the streets, headed by a drum major dressed in red trimmings and a woolly hat.
> Yesterday the buffalo observed the Simon Com-

pany's Hussar band parading the streets, and took exceptions. With head down and tail up, it charged that band. The music ceased with the first bellow of that animal, and the band done some excellent running. It was the worse broke up parade you ever saw. The buffalo took possession of the street, while the band roosted on fences, porches, and small shanties.

By far the most memorable spectacle in Dodge, however, was the "genuine Spanish bullfight" that took place on July 4, 1884, first of its kind to be held on American soil. The event was the brainchild of Mayor Ab Webster, enthusiastically supported by Ham Bell. Though a reform mayor, Webster deplored the decline in the cattle drives and the cowboy population which had led to a proportionate decline in the old-time zest and boisterous high spirits which had brought big spenders into Dodge. Carried perhaps too far, reform had subdued the city. Something sensational was needed to restore Dodge to its proud position as Queen of Western Cowtowns.

With ten thousand dollars raised by subscription, a bull ring was erected on the Fair Grounds between the Plaza and the river. Webster and Bell arranged through a Mexican lawyer to secure five part-time bullfighters from Chihuahua. Veteran cattleman Doc Barton offered to supply twelve of the most ferocious bulls from his extensive herd, though how the selection was made remained a secret. To add local interest to the contest, the bulls were named for town saloons and personalities, such as "Dog Kelley," "Long Branch," and "Ringtailed Snorter"— the latter apparently referring to one of the scrappier, hard-drinking cowboys of the town.

The advance publicity surpassed ex-mayor Webster's expectations. The press expressed outrage that such a barbarous spectacle should be held within the borders of the United States. From the pulpit, ministers deplored "this stench in the nostrils of civilization." The head of the national S.P.C.A. appealed by wire to Governor George W. Glick of Kansas: "In the name of humanity I appeal to you to prevent the contemplated bullfight at Dodge City. Let not American soil be polluted by such atrocities." The United States district attorney wired Webster that the fight was against the laws of the United States. Webster allegedly wired back: "Hell! Dodge City ain't *in* the United States."

Came the glorious Fourth and Dodge was keyed to a high pitch of excitement. The Santa Fe ran special trains bringing spectators and newspaper correspondents from miles around. Front Street was jammed with cowboys in their white felt hats and jangling spurs. Gamblers and tinhorns crowded the saloons, where heavy bets were wagered on the *corrida*. To add excitement to the occasion a traditional gunfight took place in the Alhambra, where a gambler named Dave St. Clair shot and killed a Texas drover in old-time Western style.

At midafternoon Ab Webster, accompanied by the
Cowboy Band, led the parade which preceded the
colorfully costumed matadors to the arena. The
grandstand was filled to capacity, the weather was
perfect, the crowd enthusiastic. But, alas, the fight
itself was something of a bust! The first bull, Ringtailed Snorter, was engaged by chief matador Gre-
gorio Gallardo, and for half an hour they chased each
other around the ring without making serious con-
tact. Bull and matador were finally withdrawn to
rest up for the next encounter, though there was
trouble persuading the reluctant bull to leave the
ring.

Throughout the performance the hooting, cheer-
ing audience plainly sided with the bulls. For the
Longhorns at least were natives of the Plains, fighting for Dodge City's honor, while the Mexican matadors were aliens who, to the town's disgust, refused
to take a drink before the fight.

But the next four bulls to enter the arena were a
disappointment. Like Ferdinand, they did not want
to fight—fleeing and hiding from the matadors whenever and wherever possible. In response to the disap-
proving catcalls, Ringtailed Snorter, who at least
appeared to know what he was there for, was
brought back into the fray. The plucky bull almost
succeeded in goring his opponent before Gallardo
managed to stick him with his sword.

The second day was a repetition of the first. One

bull was stabbed and hauled out of the ring, but some days later the animal was seen contentedly grazing with Doc Barton's herd, apparently unaffected by the ordeal. While the whole affair, at least in retrospect, was something of a letdown, Dodge City was grateful for this brief revival of its old-time reputation as a sportive, rough-and-tumble town where anything could happen. Other Kansas cities sought to imitate Dodge's bid for fame, Caldwell for one, but the fights were considered tame affairs. "The mad bulls that we had heard so much about," wrote a local editor, "didn't have life enough to brush the flies off."

But the fight was scarcely over when Dodge returned to its unfamiliar but developing respectability. According to Stanley Vestal, it was the following night when a disillusioned reporter asked a resident: "What's happened to your dance halls and saloons? Where's all the fun and music that I used to hear?"

"There's no music any more outside the church melodeon," the other sorrowfully told him. "The Santa Fe Railroad wants us to clean the place up if they're going to keep on running trains to Dodge. I wouldn't stay myself except that I have to play the organ twice a week in church."

Truly, the turbulent days of "anything goes" were waning.

14

Dodge City Besieged

When we reached Dodge City we drew our four
    months' pay;
  Times were better then, boys, than they are today;
The way we drank and gambled and threw the girls
    around,
  "Say, a bunch of Texas boys has come to take the
    town!"

John Garner's Trail Herd

In the so-called cattle kingdoms of the Southwest
there were many masters—one might even call them
kings—each with his loyal band of followers or trail
hands enlisted by his foreman and supported by the
monthly wages he paid. In their own domains in
Texas they were emperors. No one challenged their
authority; they were wealthy, strong-willed characters who brooked no interference. When they arrived
in the Kansas cowtowns ahead of their herds, they
exerted or tried to exert the same authority. They

didn't class themselves as visitors, in town on business, but as temporary owners of the city—men whose wealth and private cowboy armies gave them rights above the law.

Merchants and businessmen of Dodge, as well as proprietors of dance halls and saloons, were inclined to bow to this authority. After all, the cattle barons were their major source of income. The money their cowboys spent on gambling and liquor, plus that which the cattlemen themselves dispersed for such amusements, was the basis of the town's prosperity. If gross liberties were taken, if the cowboys often went too far in shooting up the streets and generally ignoring local laws, the average citizen was apt to look the other way.

But what of the city marshals and the county sheriffs who were charged with keeping law and order? Often they tried to be lenient when they could, and tactful when they couldn't, giving the cowboy and cattleman as much rope as the law allowed. But inevitably, in the boom years of the cattle drives, the two groups clashed—like opposing armies on the field of battle.

On one side were the cattle barons like the Mifflin clan, owners of the vast King Ranch of Texas, which survives today; Shanghai Pierce, a stubborn ex-New England Yankee, one of the wealthiest cattlemen of all; Tobe Driskill and his band of trigger-happy cowboys. Opposed to them were a handful of peace of-

ficers and deputies with whatever gun-skilled locals
they could deputize on instant notice. Some towns,
like Wichita, had a triangle-shaped gong hanging
near the city hall, which could be sounded to rally
the citizens to the town's defense. But Dodge disdained relying on a citizen militia. Its lawmen preferred to keep control within their own unwavering,
but dangerously outnumbered, hands.

The big test came in the peak year of 1878, when
the later-named Battle for Dodge City climaxed the
town's tempestuous career. But the seeds were sown
earlier. War between the Texas herders and the lawmen had been brewing since the spring of 1877,
when the vanguard of northbound cattle began arriving in Dodge City—265,000 Longhorns with 1300
cowboys and 250 owners. The shooting of Ed Masterson in March had added to the arrogance of this invading army. They had successfully done away with
one marshal; they felt free to hurrah the town in
good old frontier style. Several gunfights added to
the population of Boot Hill, to a point where the
city authorities declared a ban on further burials
at the site and opened a new cemetery south of
town to provide for future victims.

Dodge itself was split by rival factions in its midst.
Mayor Jim Kelley's cohorts, known disparagingly as
the Kelley gang, stood ostensibly for law and order.
In spite of the fact that Kelley was half owner of
the Alhambra Saloon, the Opera House, and other

establishments dependent on the cowboy trade, he was wise enough to recognize that unbridled lawlessness could, in the long run, ruin business. As a result, he had always supported Wyatt Earp, and had summoned Wyatt back to Dodge after "Little Ed" Masterson was slain.

In opposition to this group were the men who did business directly with the cattle barons, such as Charlie Rath, Ab Webster, H. M. Beverley, and above all, Beverley's partner Bob Wright, now a member of the Kansas state legislature, who, in spite of his exalted position in the town, seemed to put business ahead of principles. Wright's attitude, favored by many money-minded citizens, was applauded by the cattlemen, which made him a sort of quisling among the outnumbered lawmen of the town.

Charged with active law enforcement were some of the leading peace officers in the West: County Sheriff Charlie Bassett with his deputies Bat Masterson and Morgan Earp; Marshal Wyatt Earp with Jim Masterson and Billy Tilghman as deputies, sometimes assisted by Virgil Earp, Neal Brown, and Frank McLean. They were not many but they were experts at their job, and above all not easily intimidated.

Early that year Mayor Kelley was informed that there was a price on Marshal Earp's head. Who had put up the reward was kept a secret, but it was well known that the cattlemen resented Wyatt's uncompromising attitude toward observance of the law. Some old-timers claimed that Wyatt himself had spread the rumor as a means of enhancing his reputation as a formidable lawman. But too many attempts on the marshal's life took place to be ignored. Three shots were fired at him from behind a freight car on the railroad tracks, one piercing his high-crowned hat. Several nights later, as he entered his room on the ground floor of the Dodge House, the blast of a shotgun shattered the window frame above his head. This time he caught a glimpse of his assailant, fired from the window, and brought him down with a bullet in the leg. The gunman turned out to be an ordinary cowboy, down on his luck, who had learned from his trail boss that "a reward of a thousand dollars had been posted for anyone who could kill the marshal and make good his escape from the city's jurisdiction."

Along with these assaults on the marshal, the town was getting edgy. Two cattle clans had brought large herds to Dodge, the six Driskill brothers under the elder Tobe Driskill, and four Rachals under their older brother Bob. Either one might average thirty thousand head of cattle in a season, putting six hundred thousand dollars into circulation in Dodge City.

Tobe Driskill, celebrating a record sale of cattle, ignored the ban on carrying weapons on north Front

Street, and went on a little shooting spree, blasting out lights and windows. He paused in front of the Alhambra and shouted an obscene invitation to Mayor Kelley to come out and inspect the damage. Instead of Kelley, Wyatt Earp stepped forth, clubbed the rampaging cattleman with his Buntline Special, and heaved him half conscious into jail. That Wyatt had never fired his guns in the encounter was Tobe's ultimate humiliation. "I'd have been justified in shooting him," said Wyatt, "but he'd never live down the fact that I hadn't needed to shoot to get him down."

Since he was one of the leading cattlemen in town, there was agitation for Tobe's release. But neither Earp nor Kelley would budge; Driskill would remain in jail until he could face the judge next morning. When word of this reached the Driskill outfit camped outside of town, Tobe's foreman led a band of twenty-five defiant cowboys into town to break down the jail. With a horse saddled and ready for Tobe's escape, they secured a sledgehammer from the blacksmith shop and started battering at the door.

Wyatt Earp was there in seconds, his guns untouched in their holsters. He spoke only five words.

"Quit pounding on that lock," he said.

It was enough, said one eyewitness, "to suddenly make the street as quiet as a churchyard." Wyatt could easily have been shot from ambush, but by now his reputation made his very presence a deterrent.

The marshal singled out the foreman and directed his next remark to him. "Get out of town," he said. "And before you go, put that sledgehammer back where you got it."

The foreman nodded to his followers, and the cowboys left the city like a flock of sheep. The next day Tobe Driskill appeared in court to be fined a hundred dollars and dispatched to join his outfit.

But it was only the beginning of the Texas cattlemen's assault on Dodge and challenge to its authority. While the Driskill Clan was temporarily subdued, the Rachal brothers were still in town, whooping it up in Jim Kelley's Alhambra saloon. Bob Rachal, four sheets to the wind, took exception to the way Jim's fiddler played his favorite tune. When the violinist defended his performance, Rachal became more critical. He drew his revolver, split the man's head open with the butt, then pursued the hysterical musician down the street, the latter screaming bloody murder.

Wyatt Earp was quietly dining at Delmonico's when he heard the sound of shots. He reached the doorway in time to see the fleeing violinist bleeding profusely and shouting for help, with Rachal firing in drunken abandon at his heels.

The marshal moved between the gunman and his prey. "Drop those guns, Rachal," he commanded.

"Get the hell out of the way, marshal!" Bob said. "I'm going to kill that fiddling son of a bitch!"

Wyatt whipped out his Buntline Special and laid the barrel over Rachal's skull. The cattleman dropped unconscious, and Wyatt and Neal Brown carried him like a sack of meal toward the jail. Rachal's friends tried unsuccessfully to intervene, then appealed to Bob Wright to take action. Wright met the two marshals and their prisoner at the entrance to the jail.

"You can't lock up Rachal," he protested. "His business brings half a million dollars to this city."

In response, Wyatt and Brown heaved Rachal into the calaboose and locked the door.

"You let him out, or Dodge'll have a new marshal in twenty-four hours," Wright blustered.

Then the legislator made a fatal mistake. He tried to snatch the key from Wyatt's hand. The marshal wrapped an arm around Wright's neck, unlocked the door again, and pitched him into jail along with Rachal.

"If I'd done anything else," said Wyatt afterward, "I'd have lost whatever edge I had in Dodge. If I hadn't called Wright's bluff, those troublemakers would have taken over."

Kelley sided as usual with Earp. While Wright was released, Rachal paid the customary hundred-dollar fine for disturbing the peace. But the two

successive incidents roused the cattlemen and cowboys to open hostility. Mayor Kelley suggested that
Wyatt have a bodyguard, and several gunfighters
volunteered for the assignment, but the marshal declined their offer. He wouldn't give his enemies the
satisfaction of seeing him take precautions and, he
openly admitted, "What I wanted most of all was
the satisfaction of licking that whole outfit single-
handed."

On top of these victories over the invading Texans,
the reward of a thousand dollars on the marshal's
head was openly renewed and pressed, and Clay
Allison made his try for the prize. The results,
related elsewhere, were a total fiasco for Allison.
When he returned to Dodge some two weeks later,
ostensibly to close a cattle deal, he humbly sent
word to Wyatt asking the marshal's permission to
enter town. Permission was granted; Earp and his
would-be assassin traded a few polite words; and
Allison left the city never to return again.

At the close of that fateful season, Dodge was
still under the obstinate control of Marshal Earp
and Sheriff Masterson. But the spring of 1878 promised to top the previous year's invasion of the Texas
cattlemen and cowboys. Wrote the lyrical editor of
the *Times*, on May 4, "This far famed 'wicked city'
is decked in gorgeous attire in preparation for the
Longhorns and the opening of the cattle trade in

which Dodge City outshines all rivals. The season promises to be a remarkable one, and has stimulated the greatest measure of activity."

But as far as the forces of law and order went, the season started ominously with the killing in early April of Ed Masterson by Alf Walker and Jack Wagner. The marshal's elimination threatened a take-over of the town by the Texas cowboys. The editor of the *Globe* complained, "Some of the boys in direct violation of the city ordinances carry firearms on our streets without being called to account for same. They do so in such an open manner that it doesn't seem possible that our city officers are in ignorance of the fact."

Ed's death left his brother Bat Masterson almost alone in his battle with the visiting cowboys intent on taking over Dodge by the sheer superiority of numbers. But the situation was reversed by the return of Wyatt Earp in May in response to the urgent pleas of Mayor Kelley. Wyatt promptly resorted to his practiced tactics. The first two cowboys he met who refused to surrender their guns were buffaloed and hauled unconscious to the jail. One by one, every other miscreant who defied the marshal met with the same fate.

"I disliked beating up the general run of cowboys," Earp recorded. "But at that particular time their long period of license had made the whole crowd so unruly that the only way to get the situation in hand was to knock out every man who looked at me twice." The *Globe* supported his efforts, noting on May 14:

> Wyatt Earp, the most efficient officer Dodge has ever had, has just returned from Texas. . . . Hurry up with that new cemetery.

Again it was open season for gunning down Dodge City lawmen. In one of the most senseless and unprovoked killings in the history of Dodge, a drunken cowboy named Tom O'Hara snatched the revolver of Deputy Marshal Harry McCarty, who was peacefully chatting with friends in the Long Branch, and shot the officer through the groin, wounding him mortally. The murderer was himself shot by irate bystanders, but lived to face trial and conviction for murder, and sentenced to twelve years in the penitentiary.

Wyatt Earp, however, remained the principal target for Texas gunmen anxious to collect the price on his head. A few weeks later Eddie Foy and his partner Jim Thompson, along with singer Dora Hand, were performing at the Comique Theater on the South Side. Perhaps sensing trouble, Wyatt stationed himself at the door of the theater. The accounts of what happened next, by the marshal and by Eddie Foy, are somewhat contradictory.

Galloping down Front Street came a lone, determined cowboy later identified as George Hoyt from

Texas. As he drew abreast of Wyatt Earp, his forty-five roared and sent three bullets whistling past the marshal and on through the thin wall of the Comique. According to Eddie Foy, performing on the stage while others drank and gambled in the auditorium, "We were going merrily on with the dance when suddenly, Bang! Bang! Bang! came the roar of eight or ten big pistols from the outer darkness, the crash of glass from our windows and shrieks from the women." Perhaps Eddie's sense of the dramatic got the better of him, or he genuinely believed that the building had been assaulted by an army. His report continued:

> Everybody dropped to the floor at once, according to custom. Bat Masterson was in the act of dealing a game of Monte with Doc Holliday, and I was impressed by the instantaneous manner in which they flattened out like pancakes on the floor. . . . The firing kept up until it seemed to me that the assailants had put hundreds of shots through the building. . . . The marvelous part of the whole affair was that aside from a few harmless scratches and some perforated clothing, nobody in the dance hall was hurt.

Foy insisted that he also heard a barrage of bullets from the streets, where a hastily summoned posse was counterattacking, driving the band of gunmen across the river. But Wyatt Earp records simply a duel between himself and the rampaging cowboy as he chased Hoyt across the toll bridge and brought him down with a bullet in the back. Carried back to jail, George Hoyt was found by Dr. McCarty to be mortally wounded—the only fatal shooting in Wyatt Earp's professional career.

Regarding the victim, Stuart Lake recorded:

> The cowboy, it appeared, had come to Dodge a fugitive from Texas justice. Hoyt said that certain influential cattlemen had promised him that if he killed Wyatt Earp, the Texas warrant against him would be quashed and that he would be paid one thousand dollars. With this assertion on his lips, he died.

Scarcely a week had passed before another gunman named Tom Owens took two shots at the marshal as he walked along the street, then fled across the toll bridge. Unscathed, Wyatt galloped in pursuit and caught up with his assailant hiding in Dutch Henry's camp of rustlers just outside the town. He disarmed the gang and took their guns with him as he herded Owens back to jail. While Owens was fined a hundred dollars the following morning, Bat Masterson protested to Wyatt that he was too lenient with his would-be murderers. Perhaps he was, but neither Owens nor Dutch Henry's gang was ever seen in Dodge again.

In mid-September two of Wyatt's dedicated enemies, Tobe Driskill and Ed Morrison, were camped just west of Dodge with a band of twenty-five Texas

cowmen. About to leave for the season, they made a
last attack upon the city, "taking Dodge by surprise,
shooting up the South Side honkytonks, shaking up
sacrosanct Front Street, high-tailing the citizenry,
and otherwise disporting themselves in such forty-
five-caliber pleasantries as opportunity and a few
drinks might inspire."

Before Wyatt Earp had time to reach the scene
virtually every lamp and almost every pane of glass
on Front Street had been shattered. But there were
lights still burning in the Long Branch, where Frank
Loving was dealing the cards to the ever-present
gambler Doc Holliday. The marshal headed for the
saloon to see what all the shooting was about. He
met the Morrison-Driskill gang about to invade this
last remaining stronghold and climax their rampage
by shooting up the joint.

The Texans stopped short at sight of the marshal;
they had been led to believe that he was out of
town with the posse pursuing Chief Dull Knife and
his fugitive Cheyennes.

"By God, it's Wyatt Earp!" shouted Tobe Driskill.
"You white-livered bastard, you! Get ready to say
your prayers before I finish you!"

Wyatt felt he didn't have a chance. Twenty-five
liquor-reckless cowboys, each with a pair of drawn
revolvers, had him covered. If he reached for his
guns he might get a few of them, but barring a
miracle he was as good as dead. At that instant the

door of the Long Branch slapped open and a hoarse voice shouted: "Throw 'em up!"

Astonished, the cowboys turned to see Doc Holliday with a six-gun in each hand. Earp was quick to take advantage of the distraction. Whipping out his Buntline Specials he leveled them at Driskill's head, calling on the cowboys to drop their guns or their leader would be dead. The revolvers clattered to the wooden sidewalk as the Texans raised their hands. But off to one side a single cowboy took a desperate chance. Gun still in hand he took a pot shot at the marshal, when a six-gun exploded close to Wyatt's ear. The cowboy went spinning to the ground. Doc Holliday, as it was well known, never missed.

"What'll we do with the rest of 'em, Marshal?" Doc asked calmly.

In those few tense seconds the tide of battle turned for good. The siege of Dodge by the lawless hordes of cattlemen was lifted. Never again would Wyatt Earp's authority, or that of any of his deputies, be seriously challenged. Driskill and his gang were jailed, fined, ordered to leave town—and did; while the friendship between Wyatt Earp and the lawless Holliday was lastingly cemented.

There were many, Bat Masterson among them, who were puzzled by the friendly admiration the marshal had for Holliday. The two men couldn't have been less alike. But as Wyatt himself expressed it, "No one could understand the feeling that I have for Doc unless he had stood in my shoes that night as Doc came through the doorway of the Long Branch. If anyone questions the motives of my loyalty to Doc, well, there's the answer."

Wrote the editor of the *Globe* some weeks after this encounter, "The Comique Theater is closed for the season. The hurrah-look which pervaded our streets is gone, and we now linger in peace. It looks like a slow winter." But it was never slow in Dodge. Already another war was brewing.

15

The Battle of the Bottles

Whoopee! Drink that rot gut, drink that red nose,
   Whenever you get to town;
Drink it straight, and swig it mighty,
   Till the world goes round and round.

Cowboy Drinking Song

It was Dodge City's man of many parts, Bob Wright, who allegedly christened the town "the Beautiful Bibulous Babylon of the Frontier," and the name stuck, along with many less flattering titles given to this Queen of Cowtowns.

Beautiful she was not, but bibulous she was, with one saloon to every fifty inhabitants, housed in almost every other building on the Plaza. Ever since George Hoover opened his wholesale liquor store in a sod house on the site of Buffalo City, the saloon was the center of the social life, and even much of the business life, of Dodge.

Especially in the first half decade, this was understandable. The city had no YMCA, no community center, no social or athletic clubs. The saloon was the cowboy's fraternity house, the cattleman's office, the gambler's place of business, the gunman's rendez-vous. Not coincidentally many bars were owned or operated by political leaders or lawmen of the city. A. J. Peacock and Jim Kelley, the town's early mayors, were proprietors at one time or another of the Saratoga and Alhambra, George Hoover and Bat Masterson had an interest in the Alamo and the Lady Gay respectively, Billy Tilghman and Ham Bell were both saloon men, Charlie Bassett was once proprietor of the Long Branch. So it went.

There was no conflict of interest in these opera-tions. By running a saloon the marshal or city official was in constant touch with town affairs. His office, generally a table near the bar, was in dead center of the mainstream of events, a position in which he could keep abreast of what transpired in the town. The system had worked well in Wichita for Wild Bill Hickok, who rarely left his table in the Bull's Head Tavern, and it worked well for Dodge City marshals. Wyatt Earp never touched liquor, but he often patronized the Long Branch and the other bars and gambling saloons as a means of knowing who was in town and what they might be up to.

In the early days raw whiskey was the sole libation. Before the coming of the Santa Fe, beer was too bulky and costly to be freighted to the frontier towns. And the stronger the bite the more popular the drink, regardless of how it tasted. A man who could not down a tumbler of raw whiskey without pausing to catch his breath was considered lacking in virility, while those who did not drink at all, like Wyatt Earp, sometimes had to defend with their fists the right to refuse the offer of a glass of red-eye.

The whiskey that first was peddled from the wagon tailboards of itinerant liquor peddlers was all but lethal. Raw alcohol was colored with coffee and flavored with ground pepper to increase its sting. One whiskey vendor named Thompson was noted for the head-splitting potency of his product. A jealous competitor sneaked a look at one of his kegs and discovered the secret of his formula. A half-dozen rattlesnake heads were found in the bottom of the barrel. Thompson's "snakehead whiskey" became famous on the cowtown trail.

But as Dodge matured, more genteel drinking habits were observed and the saloons acquired a veneer of elegance. Wines, brandies, and champagne were offered. Beer was freighted into town by railroad, and the press reported the cowboy's favorite brand as being "Miss Ann Heuser with the long, thin neck so pleasant to embrace."

The Long Branch was the largest and most profitable public house in Dodge. Opened by Charlie Bassett in 1873, it was later owned by Chalkley Beeson and W. H. Harris. Considered "artistically functional" by one discerning critic, it offered a bit of everything: a lengthy bar for serving drinks, gambling tables, music, entertainment, dancing. On busy nights the swinging doors were kept propped open, as were the doors of other saloons, to expedite the traffic.

While patrons were obliged to check their guns before entering a North Side bar or gambling house, the rules were easy to evade, and the saloons became scenes of frequent violence, often headquarters of rival factions. After the Earps and Mastersons quit Dodge in the fall of 1879, leaving Jim Masterson as Bat's surrogate at the Lone Star Saloon, trouble developed over a bartender named Al Updegraph, brother-in-law of A. J. Peacock. After some months of dwindling receipts, Jim began suspecting Updegraph of dipping his hand into the till.

Updegraph retaliated with the charge that he was being framed; that, in fact, Jim was doling out money to one of his dance-hall girls and trying to force Updegraph to keep the matter secret. Jim then told his partner Peacock that Updegraph would have to go. Whatever the truth of the matter was, the saloon habitués—eager to promote a quarrel promising diversion—quickly took up their respective cudgels, some siding with Peacock and his kinsman barkeep, others siding with Jim Masterson.

As tension grew, Jim felt that even with the badge of marshal he was facing something he couldn't handle. He wired Bat Masterson for help. Bat was in Tombstone, dealing faro for Wyatt Earp in the latter's highly successful Oriental Gambling Saloon, in which Luke Short was also involved. Bat took the next train to Dodge, arriving on Saturday, April 16. He anticipated trouble and was fully armed.

As Bat walked across the Plaza looking for Jim, he caught sight of Peacock and Updegraph on the south side of the square. He called to them, suggesting that they talk things over. Instead of responding, the two saloon men ducked behind the heavily timbered jail and opened fire. Bat dropped behind the slightly elevated railroad tracks in the center of Front Street, and returned the fire. Thus began what was later known as the famous Battle of the Plaza.

So many shots were fired in the subsequent half hour that nobody could keep count. Once the battle was engaged, it seemed as if the whole town joined the fray on one side or another. Windows were shattered on both sides of Front Street, and the pall of smoke that obscured the Plaza turned high noon to graveyard dusk. Yet only one bullet found its mark, plowing through Updegraph's lung but not, surprisingly, proving fatal. When Bat and his cohorts started running out of ammunition, causing a lull in the hostilities, Mayor Ab Webster strode out to the tracks with a twelve-gauge shotgun and arrested Bat.

Bat was brought to trial and pleaded guilty. He

was fined eight dollars and ordered to leave town. He persuaded Jim that the Mastersons were running out of friends in Dodge; it was time to move on to greener pastures. The brothers dissolved their partnership with A. J. Peacock, and Jim turned in his marshal's badge. They later ended up in Trinidad, Colorado, where they leased and ran a gambling saloon.

If the Battle of the Plaza failed to reach the proportions of a major war, it was a preview of conflicts yet to come. For the saloons were a sacred institution in the Kansas cowtowns, the castles of contention, each with its loyal band of patron-followers. Moreover, Luke Short had arrived in town. Whether or not he arrived in time to take part in the initial strife is not recorded. But he came with ambitions that would once again make Dodge a battleground.

Trouble had been brewing for some time in the spring of 1883. "Wars and rumors of war, was the outcry all along the line," reported the Ford County *Globe* on May 1. The editor attributed the "smouldering volcano" to an "Ordinance for the Suppression of Vice and Immorality in Dodge City" and to another measure "to Define and Punish Vagrancy" passed by the town council a week earlier. However, had a less tempestuous character than Luke Short been the center of attention, the situation might never have developed into what old-timers

later called The Great Saloon War or The Second
Battle for Dodge City.

Luke had returned to Dodge that spring, loaded
with his winnings from dealing faro at Wyatt Earp's
saloon in Tombstone. He had previously supervised
the gambling operations in the Long Branch. Now he
was able to buy out Chalk Beeson's interest in that
saloon, sharing its ownership with Will Harris, a
generally affable and easygoing partner.

Next door to the Long Branch was the Alamo,
owned by Mayor Ab Webster. Webster was not only
a business competitor; he hated both Bill Harris and
Luke Short and there had been a running feud among
the three for several years. Webster had been elected
mayor on the "reform" ticket—meaning that he was
ostensibly opposed to gambling and other questionable activities in the city. The fact that he ran a gambling saloon himself was typical of the inconsistent,
often crazy, system of politics in Dodge.

At the end of his term, Webster nominated Larry
Deger to succeed him. He was supported by the
influential Bob Wright, Wright's business partner
H. M. Beverley, and saloon man Ham Bell. The opposition, led by Jim Kelley and representing the more
sporting-minded of the town, nominated Luke Short's
partner, Billy Harris. The city was thus divided into
rival camps, Larry Deger's party advocating a crack-
down on the dance halls, gambling parlors, and saloons; Bill Harris standing for these same wide-open

wickedest little city in the world."

The election for mayor was a farce. The Santa operations which had brought such fame and wealth to Dodge and had led to its proud position as "the Fe Railroad, which was anxious to see the town cleaned up, surreptitiously imported trainmen and work crews who rushed to the polls to vote for Larry Deger. Deger was supported too by the fiery editor of the *Times*, Nicholas B. Klaine, who assured his readers that with Harris as mayor "the town would become a snug harbor for all the robbers, drunks, con men, and general ne'er-do-wells in the area." As a consequence, when the vote was counted, Deger had defeated Harris by 214 to 143.

In spite of the rigged election, things might have continued peacefully enough if it had not been for the business rivalry between the Long Branch and the Alamo. The new mayor was simply a mouthpiece for Ab Webster, and his opposition to gambling applied only to Luke Short's establishment, with the aim of putting the Long Branch out of business. Short's association with the Long Branch thus became, as one wag put it, the "Long and Short of it," the crux of the ensuing war.

Though gambling under the "reform" administration was booming as never before, Luke Short wanted more than a lion's share of the business. He was inspired to hire a comely female piano player from Kansas City, whose lively airs, echoing on the Plaza through the open doors and windows of the Long Branch, had the cowboys swarming into Luke's saloon like bees to honey. The Alamo lost business in proportion as the Long Branch gained it. Webster decided something must be done. He persuaded Larry Deger to pass an ordinance forbidding female performers in saloons. The mayor did.

Luke Short was not yet ready to buck the mayor. Complying with the new law he discharged his piano player, only to learn that twenty-four hours later she was playing at the Alamo! She had proved so popular at the Long Branch that Luke's cowboy customers shifted their patronage to the neighboring saloon. Luke promptly retaliated by hiring another alluring piano player along with a string quartet to drown out the strains of music from the Alamo. Immediately Mayor Deger sent several deputies, including C. L. Hartman, to haul the offending musicians into jail on the ground of disturbing the peace.

Attached to a short fuse, Luke's temper was close to exploding. That night, strolling down the Plaza to the music from the Alamo, he crossed paths with deputy Hartman. Hartman saw him first. Perhaps reflecting the general jitteriness of Dodge, he drew his gun and fired. The shot went wild. Luke whipped out his forty-four and let go at Hartman. The deputy tried to run, stumbled, and fell as two bullets creased his hair. Convinced that he had killed the deputy, Luke retreated to the Long Branch and with the help of loyal customers barricaded the doors and windows. Luke made it plain to the outside that they would defend the fortress to the last man.

Next morning, Larry Deger's officers persuaded Luke to abandon his fortified position. They assured him Hartman had not been killed; no charges of murder had been filed; and Short was free to walk the streets and put the Long Branch back in operation. It was all that Luke wanted, to protect the life's savings he'd invested in the Long Branch and to carry on business as before. Unaware of a trap, Luke threw the doors open and was immediately swamped by deputies and carried off to jail along with five of his supporters.

They were not long in jail. The next day, seemingly drunk with power, Larry Deger's gorillas hauled the prisoners to the Santa Fe depot and gave them their choice of trains going east or west. One stipulation: any who returned to Dodge would be shot on sight. Luke took the train for Kansas City.

Luke's partner, Billy Harris, was not among those exiled. But he came so close to being included that he dared not raise a hand against the obvious injustice of the mayor's move. Even the press began to look askance at Deger's dictatorial tactics. It was not so much the antisaloon measures that he imposed, but the partiality with which they were applied; they were only enforced against Deger's or ex-mayor Webster's competitors. When a lawyer representing the refugees arrived in Dodge to plead their collective case, he was driven back aboard the train with a shotgun at his head.

The *Globe* now reported that the situation in Dodge was critically dangerous. "The smouldering volcano threatens to burst forth in all its fury." Tom Nixon, who operated a dance hall and saloon with Brick Bond, organized a group of vigilantes known as the Shotgun Brigade. They stood guard at the depot, and even mounted the Santa Fe trains to make certain none of the exiles would return. One who attempted to do so and started disembarking at the station stared into a battery of twelve-gauge shotguns leveled at his face. He wasted no time in getting back into the car.

Up to now Luke Short had shown extraordinary patience and restraint. Now he was fighting mad. He took two bold and well-considered steps. The first was to carry his case directly to Governor George W. Glick of Kansas. Considering that Luke Short was a well-known gambler with a record of many brushes with the law, Glick's regard for justice does him lasting credit. He listened to Luke's story, was persuaded of its accuracy, and telegraphed Ford County sheriff George T. Hinkel demanding a rundown on the situation. Hinkel, as the mayor's appointee, was a stooge for Deger. He wired back that Short and his associates had been banished from Dodge because they threatened the peace of the city, and that, as a result, all now was quiet and no interference by the governor was needed.

Reading between the lines, Glick again showed his mettle. He let loose an ear-scorching blast at Webster's and Deger's forces referring to Luke Short's expulsion as an "outrage" and the state of affairs at Dodge as "monstrous." Events "simply show that the mayor is unfit for his position," and "the disgrace that is being brought upon Dodge City must be wiped out." He labeled the dispute for what it was, "simply a difficulty between saloon men and dance halls," with the mayor and his marshal conniving to drive their competitors out of business. If the matter was not corrected he, the governor, would send troops to Dodge to impose martial law, and establish a new municipal administration.

Before Mayor Deger's Front Street boys had time to receive and digest this ultimatum, Luke Short had taken the second step in his campaign. He wired Bat Masterson in Denver and Wyatt Earp in Silverton to join him in his planned assault on the establishment in Dodge. Masterson took the next train to Kansas City, Wyatt rounded up a band of gunmen and headed for Kinsley, Kansas, a convenient beachhead for his expeditionary force.

The occupation of the town took place with all the secrecy and careful timing by resistance movements in wars throughout the world. On May 13 the local paper noted the sudden presence of the freedom fighters, armed to the teeth, occupying strategic points around the city. It warned of a "terrible tragedy" impending, and mentioned the invading principals by name: Bat Masterson, "killer of at least a dozen men"; Wyatt Earp "equally famous in the cheerful business of depopulating the country"; Charlie Bassett, Rowdy Joe Lowe, Shotgun Collins, and worse than all, "the infamous Doc Holliday." The reporter mentioned the presence of others he could not identify. They were the gunslingers that constituted Wyatt Earp's elite battalion of shock troops.

The rumors flew fast and thick. Governor Glick had reportedly sent fifty armed troopers to Dodge to pave the way for Luke Short's return. The governor denied this; he had simply advised the sheriff to recruit a citizen's militia to ensure the safety of its returning citizens. There was a conspiracy afoot to assassinate Luke Short. U. S. Adjutant General Thomas H. Moonlight arrived in Dodge to check out this possibility. Moonlight telegraphed the governor, "Short can be protected from public attack but not from private assault." He added, "The sheriff is earnest but should excitement continue he cannot secure men to do his bidding."

With both factions held in perilous check, like bulldogs straining at the leash, Wyatt Earp made his move. He posted his henchmen, along with Bat Masterson, Charlie Bassett, and Doc Holliday, at

strategic points around the Plaza, then summoned
the City Council for a conference. It was not so
much a discussion as a statement of his demands.
In blunt words he summarized the situation and
told the council what was what. Luke Short, he said,
at his request, was on his way to Dodge; and he
added:

> He'll stay in Dodge as long as he wants to, to
> continue business, or close out. If Ab Webster has a
> woman piano player, Luke Short can have one. If
> Luke can't have one, no one else can. I have four
> friends in town with me. We're here to see that Luke
> gets an even break, and we can stay indefinitely.

Perhaps it was Wyatt Earp's commanding, square-
jawed presence that caused the enemy to knuckle
under. The Council agreed that Luke Short could
return to Dodge, with all his rights restored. It was
useless for Deger to protest. He tried to add the
codicil that Luke was welcome only if his armed
gorillas left the city—the gorillas being Masterson,
Bassett, Earp, and Holliday and Earp's quartet of
gunmen. The mayor's suggestion was ignored.

No Shakespearean actor ever made a more tri-
umphant entrance on the stage than did Luke Short
on stepping off the train at Dodge on Sunday afternoon, June 3. He was given a conquering hero's welcome at the depot by his allies. All marched beneath
watching eyes to the Long Branch, their field headquarters, for a toast to victory. Mayor Deger had

put a temporary ban on gambling, and for once the order was obeyed. Luke's return from exile, like Napoleon's return from Elba, called for no additional diversion.

As often happens in the case of military victory, Mayor Deger's supporters quickly shifted their allegiance to the winning side. Deger was suddenly without a friend. He had gone too far, the town asserted, in imposing his will upon the gambling fraternity. Gambling was a sacred institution in the town, as were the dance-hall girls whom visiting cattlemen relied upon for entertainment. Dodge's salvation lay in once again becoming the wide-open town it used to be, where "anything goes" was the prevailing rule.

As a crowning touch, Luke Short swore out a complaint against the police official who had jailed him, and then sued the city for fifteen thousand dollars in damages for false arrest and personal injury. The suit was settled out of court. Mayor Deger was shortly replaced in office by former mayor George M. Hoover. Not only were all dance halls and gambling saloons restored to full operation, but, just for the hell of it, a new one was opened to accommodate the boom in business. The shoe was on the other foot, and though the citizens' militia known as Glick's Guards still patrolled the streets, their loyalty was now to Short's contingent.

A final outcome to this Donnybrook was the for-

mation of the famous "peace commission." While
the group photograph of this commission, reproduced
elsewhere, is the best pictorial record of great Western lawmen in existence, it has been sorely mis-
represented in the histories of the West. It was not,
as is often reported, a governing body to impose a
new administration on the city. The picture itself is
simply a memorable record of the winning combination akin to team photographs so popular in college
dormitories.

The eight-man group, which the *Times* referred to
now as "our distinguished visitors," consisted of
Wyatt Earp, Bat Masterson, Charlie Bassett, William
Harris, Luke Short, Frank McClean, former assistant
marshal Neal Brown, and Billy Petillon, editor of
the Dodge City *Democrat*, all ardent supporters of
Luke Short in the controversy. When the photograph
was developed, it showed all eight with somewhat
grim, belligerent expressions. One of the group suggested, tongue in cheek, labeling it the "peace commission," and the name was cherished throughout
local history like the inscription on a monument.
The commission did, however, leave the city better
off. It installed, as marshal, the incorruptible Billy
Tilghman, one of the best lawmen Dodge had ever
had.

So ended the Great Saloon War or the Battle of
the Bottles. Mission accomplished, Wyatt Earp's
forces quit the city on June 10, leaving Luke Short

reinstated at the Long Branch. But as someone has pointed out, it is hard to forgive a man you've wronged, and Luke found the town a shade inhospitable. He had proved his point, he had saved the Long Branch, and everything that happened now would be an anticlimax. That fall Luke sold his interest in the famed saloon to his partner, Billy Harris, and moved on to Fort Worth, Texas, and to further fame of a less creditable sort.

Peace settled over Dodge. And though there were those reluctant to admit it, the city was becoming tame. It still had plenty of vitality to weather the winds of change. But change, it knew, was coming.

16

To Beat the Devil

Amazing grace, how sweet the sound
That saved a wretch like me!
I once was lost, but now I'm found,
Was blind, but now I see.
Early Western spiritual

Sunday, November 13, 1872.

No church bells sounded over Dodge on that autumn sabbath. There were no such bells to sound. The city, under its new name, was barely three months old, and a church would have seemed incongruous among the squalid dance halls and saloons that mushroomed along Front Street.

But the strains of "Bringing In the Sheaves" resounded from the lobby of the Dodge House, where S. A. Newell, trainman with the Santa Fe, had coaxed six children to join him in hymn singing. This, the first religious enterprise in Dodge, was interrupted only when the guests complained that the noise disturbed their sleep. The Pied Piper of Dodge then moved his disciples to a new location, and the services continued.

"God came to Dodge City in 1872," wrote one who was familiar with those earliest of times. But Newell was more modest in his own assessment of his efforts. He reported only:

> The leaven is working. Have tried to get the religious elements united to sustain worship, and have obtained the names of all religious people, thirteen in all. Have tried to get a preacher there, but have not had much success.

It would be two years before this goal was reached. Meanwhile, religion in Dodge City was a hit-or-miss affair. There were itinerant preachers drifting into town from time to time, some of them gamblers in disguise who used their ecclesiastic vestments as a decoy to attract unwary players to their tables. And there were Sankey and Moody-type evangelists who, with threats of fire and brimstone, softened up the sinner for his brief conversion. Wrote Western commentator Lucius Beebe:

> Entertainment and social life were rare on the Great Plains . . . and revival meetings conducted by itinerant evangelists were looked forward to as an emotional release and social gathering. Their excesses were many and the immorality induced by their hysterical atmosphere eventually brought them into disrepute in respectable communities.

This is not to say that there was no spiritual life in Dodge beneath the callous surface of its rough existence. In homes throughout the burgeoning city the family Bible occupied the same position of importance as the patent-medicine almanac, the latter promoting miraculous cures that rivaled Lazarus's resurrection from the dead. Women, particularly, felt the need for a faith to cling to in the hard lives they were forced to lead.

And the cowboys who made up such a large part of the shifting population were far more religious than they would admit. In the century to follow there arose a wartime saying, "There are no atheists in the trenches." One could say with equal truth, "There were no atheists on the Plains." Ordinarily arrogant, blasphemous, and intemperate—ready to break any of the Ten Commandments when he hit town—the cowboy on the vast and lonely prairie was moved by a religious awe. Many carried Bibles in their saddlebags, and not a few could recite the Psalms from memory.

When nightfall blotted out the far horizon and the campfire seemed a tiny pinpoint on the fringe of eternity, the talk around the fire often segued from the ribald to the reverent. The light songs such as "Oh, Susannah!" yielded to hymns and spirituals, with often a mumbled prayer recited jointly before turning in.

Similarly, as the night riders chosen to guard the

herd made their appointed rounds, tracing wide circles around the dozing steers, they would whistle and sing to keep the cattle calm, to let them know that guardian friends were present. And they chose, not popular melodies, but such religious classics as "Abide with Me" and "Rock of Ages"—partly perhaps to soothe the cattle, certainly to help comfort the lonely man on horseback faced with that immense and silent solitude.

Early in 1874 the Reverend J. W. Fox happened into town and was disturbed to find that "there was little or no real sentiment favoring religious matters in Dodge City." He proposed to hold a series of meetings in a frame building just off Front Street. Unfortunately for this man of the cloth the two McAfee brothers, gunmen outlaws with a penchant for baiting preachers, had a proposal of their own. They would shoot up the place if Fox went ahead with his plans.

Reverend Fox did go ahead, and a sizable congregation assembled in the building. The preacher noted the two McAfees in the audience with six-guns on their hips. He adopted precisely the one tactic that gained respect in Dodge. He walked down the aisle and confronted the two gunmen.

"I understand," he told them, "that some unsavory characters have threatened to shoot up this meeting. But I know of your reputation and I see you carry guns. I'm sure nothing of that sort will happen so long as men of your caliber are here to maintain order."

The service was held, with the proud and flattered McAfee brothers presiding as guards and monitors.

It was not until June of 1878 that Dodge saw the construction of its first church. It was the spiritual child of the Reverend O. W. Wright (no relation to Bob Wright, the somewhat opportunistic senior citizen of Dodge). Wright had been in the city since April of that year, supervising the construction of his Union Church located just a little way from Front Street. In announcing that "the wicked city of Dodge can at last boast of a Christian church," the editor of the *Times* continued:

> We would have mentioned the matter last week but we thought it best to break the news gently to the outside world. The tender bud of Christianity is only just beginning to sprout, but as "tall oaks from little acorns grow," so this infant under the guide and care of Brother Wright, may grow and spread its foliage like the manly oak of the forest. Years ago John the Baptist preached in the wilderness of Judea, and his meat was locusts and wild honey, but he baptized many converts in the River Jordan. Who can tell but that years hence another Luke may write a book about our minister preaching in the wilderness of Dodge City and baptizing converts in the river Arkansas?

Up to that moment, the nearest a Dodge City cowboy felt that he had come to organized religion was

sharing drinks in the Long Branch with Mysterious
Dave Mather, reputed to be a lineal descendant of
the Puritan revivalist Cotton Mather—a kinship
which Mysterious Dave, who had gained his nickname by revealing nothing of his past, did not deny.

At this point in Dodge City's life, crowded as it
was with buffalo hunters and a rising cowboy population, probably nobody but the Reverend Wright
could have succeeded in such a project. For Wright
had brought to Dodge a tolerant understanding of
the frontier character. In time the *Globe* would label him "one of the best and most generous men
that God ever fashioned"—a rare tribute from that
often vitriolic and sarcastic paper.

Wright collected money for building his church
in the best of all possible ways, by soliciting contributions in the town's saloons. Unprincipled gamblers
were glad to hedge their bets while wagering on the
devil; overindulgent drinkers welcomed this means
of compensating for their weakness; while gunmen,
shady ladies, and others with secret sins upon their
consciences sought hope for absolution as the hat
was passed.

More than that, the Reverend Wright enlisted the
idle muscle of the town to build the church, since
carpenters as well as wood were scarce. Freighters
brought in lumber from the northern woodlands;
Zimmermann's provided paint and hardware; blasphemous bullwhackers, mule skinners, and buffalo

hunters helped to raise the beams and shingle the tower and install the bells, which were forged by the local blacksmith.

In short, the town and its leading personalities became involved. Bat Masterson and Wyatt Earp were installed as deacons, thus guaranteeing the behavior of the congregation. As a footnote to this activity, the *Times* reported that sale of Bibles that summer in Dodge City reached four hundred dollars, "which would bear comparison to towns of lesser note."

It was not a major change in Dodge's life, simply a recognition that another side existed: the fact that "some three hundred residents could qualify as decent," living mostly north of Front Street, attending to legitimate businesses by day, and staying off the streets at night. Wrote Wyatt Earp in his memoirs, "Without any attempt at whitewashing Dodge's widely advertised iniquity, I'd like to go on record as stating that she offered a lot of fun outside her saloons and hurdy-gurdies." The marshal continued:

> It may surprise some to learn that the church supper was Dodge City's most popular institution. The town ran strongly to bachelors, and what few wives and daughters of local business men there were, followed the customs of other villages with their sewing circles, church entertainments and parties for raising church funds. We single fellows certainly turned out for a chance at good home cooking, and

usually there'd be a big delegation of Texas men on hand at the suppers for the same reason. The cowboys behaved at such times and the women made them welcome.

When the town was emptied of most of its visitors in winter months, the church groups sought other means of raising money and sustaining interest. Dodge was becoming a family town, and the Ladies' Aid Society conceived the idea of a popularity contest among infants one year old. As a money raiser, votes were sold at six for a quarter, and gambler Luke Short offered a hundred dollars in prize money for the winner. Mothers and their friends canvassed the streets, the gambling parlors, and the saloons to peddle votes. And the gambling inclinations of the city helped. Poker and faro games were held in which the winnings went for votes in behalf of this or that yearling in the race.

Dr. Wright was assigned to announce the winner at a big church supper at the contest's close. The church was packed, with every member of the audience having some stake in the winner. But as the minister tallied the count, his face was puzzled. The name of the champion was unfamiliar, both to him and to the congregation.

"I am not acquainted with this child," the preacher confessed, "but if the parents will produce him and establish his right to this purse of gold, I shall be glad to hand it over."

Deacons Masterson and Earp were assigned to bring the infant to the church, while the proud, expectant mothers twittered with excitement. Who was this dark horse? Then Masterson and Earp returned with a very plump woman of questionable reputation from the South Side with a baby two weeks old. There was no doubt that the entire gambling fraternity had hunted out and voted for this child (had even given the mother an extra ten dollars above the prize to make certain she'd be present), but if the somewhat proud and snobbish mothers and friends of mothers were chagrined, the males in the audience were delighted, and even the Reverend Wright's face wore a sly, benign grin.

When an irate mother demanded to know the father's name, "That," said the minister, "is this lady's business"—and the prize was duly awarded.

Like the frontier doctor in that climate of violence, preacher Wright was ever in the presence of sudden death. It was he who was called to administer the last rights and say the necessary words as the plain pine coffin, containing a murdered gunman, was lowered into the grave on Boot Hill. His text was consolingly the same, "The Lord giveth and the Lord taketh away," a comforting thought to the mourners in that it transferred the responsibility for sudden sometimes senseless death to other shoulders.

His, too, was the responsibility of comforting the

sick and dying, and in this he drew no social distinctions, recognizing death as the great equalizer.
When he first attended the deathbed of a scarlet
lady of the town, he was bitterly criticized by his
prudish congregation. The following Sunday his
sermon was, predictably, freighted with the message,
"Let him among you who is without sin cast the
first stone." Said one old-timer, "That sure stopped
their wagging tongues."

From time to time revivalists hit town, and pitched
tents on the outskirts or preached extemporaneously
in the saloons. Since their message generally involved abstention from liquor, gambling, and women,
it was given little heed. But one evangelist was long
remembered. Brother Johnson was said to have "a
magnetic appeal, goin' for sin all spraddled out."
He had enough appeal to persuade Rowdy Kate
Lowe to allow him to hold revival meetings in
Kate's Green Front Saloon, insisting that any smaller
amphitheater would not accommodate the many
sinners who would flock to hear him preach.

Attendance, however, was disappointing. Though
chairs had been set up facing the extemporaneous
pulpit, what patrons there were stayed close to the
bar, with their backs turned to the preacher. Two
gambling friends of Kate suggested that it was time
for Brother Johnson to perform some spiritual feat,
other than his legerdemain of hauling live snakes
from a whiskey bottle to demonstrate the lethal

quality of drink. To persuade an incurable sinner to hit the sawdust trail would be a prime attraction, drawing an appreciative audience if properly promoted. They recommended as a subject Prairie Dog Dave Morrow, agreed by consensus to be the orneriest sinner in Dodge City.

That evening, accompanied by an enthusiastic audience, Prairie Dog Dave was all but carried to the hall, where he was flanked by well-wishing guardians to see that he didn't make a break for liberty. Brother Johnson, aware of the location and identity of Dave, opened all stops, extolling the glories of the afterlife to those who lived virtuously on earth. He, Brother Johnson, did not drink, smoke, blaspheme, or commune with women, and as a result looked forward to meeting his Maker when he passed the pearly gates. To this the deacons and other members of the congregation uttered a sincere Amen!

That was too much for Dave, whose ears had been devoutly bent to every word. As an old-timer in the audience related, Dave rose from his chair and shouted: "'I've got your message, friends, and I reckon it's time to start for heaven. First the preacher, then the deacons, and me last.' Then Dave whips out a whoppin' big gun and starts shootin'. The preacher went right through a window and took it with him. He was sure in some hurry.

The deacons hunted cover. Seemed like they was willin' to postpone takin' that through ticket to heaven."

Dave belted his guns with a smug grin.

"There you are, friends!" He shouted to the cowed gathering. "That old son of a bitch ain't no more ready to die than I am!"

Apart from the itinerant "hell cheaters," or revivalists, Dodge was sometimes visited by "lecturers" proposing to bring culture and intellectual advancement to the city. While the men who risked such assignments took their lives in their hands, they hoped that sufficient curiosity might line their pockets with money dropped in the collection plate.

Andy Adams, cowhand of the Texas trails, arrived one night in Dodge when Dr. J. Graves Brown, "the noted scientist," was scheduled to speak on the occult sciences. Brown had had some experience with cowtown audiences. He engaged the Lady Gay Saloon to serve as auditorium for the sake of its congenial atmosphere, and hired Bat Masterson to protect him from hecklers, drunks, or mischief makers in the audience.

The professor had barely opened his mouth to announce that he had been invited to speak in Dodge, when someone shouted, "You lie!" The speaker flushed, but continued to state his qualifications as an authority on the occult sciences,

when the same party shouted, "That's another damn
lie!" Then, as Andy Adams recorded in his *Log of
a Cowboy:*

> Masterson came to his feet like a flash, a gun in
> each hand, saying, "Stand up, you measly skunk, so
> I can see you." Half a dozen men rose in different
> parts of the house and cut loose at him, and as they
> did so the lights went out and the room filled with
> smoke. Masterson was blazing away with two guns,
> which so lighted up the rostrum that we could see
> the professor crouching under the table. Of course
> they were using blank cartridges, but the audience
> raised the long yell and poured out through the
> windows and doors, and the lecture was over. A
> couple of police came in later, escorted the pro-
> fessor to his room in the hotel, and quietly advised
> him that Dodge was hardly capable of appreciating
> anything so advanced as a lecture on the occult
> sciences.

Following in the wake of C. W. Wright's Presbyterian Church, the Catholics organized under
Fathers Felix Swembergh and Robert Loehrer; then
the Baptists, led by the Reverend N. G. Collins.
Collins fulfilled the prophecy made by the Dodge
City *Times* in 1872, by baptizing many dripping
converts in the muddy Arkansas. Among them was
the notorious gunman Jack Allen, who had earlier
killed Frank Loving in a Colorado shoot-out.

Allen arose from the shallow waters of the river
to become a preacher in his own right, convincing

Dodge that little short of the miraculous was taking place. The city would never wear a halo, but a Stairway to Heaven could be seen among the mirages of the Plains.

17

Sunset over Dodge

There's a sigh in the heart of the Last Great West,
   A sigh for the days that are gone,
For these are the men whom the West loved best,
   The men who are passing on.

                              E. M. BOOM

Few in Dodge City would have acknowledged, in
1885, that the golden days were over, and that
Dodge was sinking into history. It had survived so
many crises in its meteoric lifetime that it seemed
unsinkable. Mere change could not destroy it; and
yet change was coming.

In the early years of that decade the cattle boom
continued, with more than three hundred thousand
head arriving in Dodge in 1884. But an outbreak of
the ever-present Spanish, or cattle, fever caused
Governor Glick to impose an embargo on further
drives of Longhorns into Kansas. County Sheriff
Patrick F. Sughrue, last of the great law officers in

Dodge and known as "Old Blue" for the gunpowder marks that marred his face, had the sad responsibility of intercepting the Texas herds coming up the Western Trail toward the city. There were still Longhorns grazing on the prairies around Dodge, most of them owned by Kansas ranchers, but more and more the domestic Shorthorns had begun to take their place.

And by 1885 the cowboy himself, who had contributed so greatly to the life of Dodge, was all but gone. Among songs of the cowboys are the eloquent verses:

> The cowboys and the Longhorns
> Who pardnered in Eighty-four
> Have gone to their last roundup
> Over on the other shore.
>
> They answered well their purpose
> But their glory must fade and go,
> Because men say there's better things
> In the modern cattle show.

The embargo on Texas cattle marked the end of an era for Dodge City, as the passing of Dodge itself as Queen of Cowtowns would end an unforgettable era in the history of the West. The Longhorns still kept coming in defiance of the law, but in dwindling numbers. Attempts to establish a government-controlled corridor, through which cattle could pass without hindrance or inspection, had collapsed. And that was not the worst of it. Sheep were now grazing on hundreds of thousands of acres, and sheep were to the cattlemen like locusts to the farmer; they ate and trampled the range grass; they even smelled obnoxious.

On top of it all, the homesteading farmers, or grangers, had moved into the Plains. The barbed wire which had been invented in 1873 was everywhere, marking out small exclusive domains which collectively covered a hundred thousand acres where cattle could not trespass. The range was no longer open. The buffalo sod had been plowed and sown to thousands of bushels of wheat, thousands of acres of waving grain. Where early passengers on the Santa Fe from Atchison to Dodge had seen, first, herds of black-robed buffalo, then thousands of grazing Longhorns, now the picture from their windows was quite different.

A correspondent for the New York *Herald*, traveling the Santa Fe to Dodge, reported: "Riding in a silver palace car one of the most impressive sights that meets the eye of the traveler through this State is this mammoth field of solid miles of grain, shining in the sunlight, ripening for the harvest, bending to the breeze and waving to and fro like a sea of molten gold."

But the gold was not the old-time gold of Dodge, that fed the wheels of chance on Front Street, tilted the bottles at the gay saloons, peopled the city with gunfighters, gamblers, and dance-hall girls. Maybe this new era was an improvement. But no Texas cowboy of that golden past would have believed it.

There were other blows to come. In March 1885, Kansas passed new laws prohibiting the sale and consumption of alcoholic beverages. In Dodge, that was like denying man the bread of life. So violent was Dodge's opposition to the law, and so flagrantly did the saloons stay open, that the state attorney general came to look the situation over. His conclusion was flattering: that Dodge City had an individuality all its own, and could not be subjected to the rules of government applied to ordinary towns. "The town will work out its own salvation," he pronounced. "It cannot be redeemed and purified by means of the lash in the hands of outside parties."

How right he was. It took one of Dodge's most admired and best-loved citizens to turn the trick and sober up the city. In an extraordinary switch, Bat Masterson, champion of frontier freedom, had gone over to the prohibition side—for what reason is unclear. In 1885 he returned to Dodge at the head of an army of prohibition agents and closed down the saloons. The great names of the past—the Long Branch, the Alhambra, the Lady Gay, the Alamo, the Green Front, and the Lone Star saloon—those castles of kings of the trail were shuttered. A few minor establishments offered "temperance" drinks which were secretly guaranteed to contain the same amount of alcohol as whiskey; and "blind pigs" opened up on side streets like Pot Alley. But it was not the Bibulous Babylon of yore.

Hog raising began to take the place of cattle raising, and in 1886, 186 carloads of hogs were shipped from Dodge. Commercial enterprise turned from cattle to grain. George Hoover, now president of the first Dodge City Bank, diversified his interests and built a flour mill near the depot. The Ford County *Globe*, which had for so long gloried in the blood-and-thunder life of Dodge, now meekly reported: "Every day wagonloads of wheat are being hauled to the new grain elevator east of the stockyards. We believe the day will come when Dodge City will rank among the great wheat-producing centers of the State." The *Globe* was right. Dodge was becoming known as "the buckle on the Kansas wheat belt."

Other, more unfortunate, changes overtook the city. Early in the winter of 1886, the first of three catastrophic fires broke out in a grocery store on the north side of Front Street. The whiskey barrels filled with water were useless to contain the flames, and with only a hose cart and hand pump for equipment, the fire brigade—which had been largely a social club for prominent citizens of the town—was helpless. Eleven city blocks were leveled to the ground.

On a cold November night, the alarm sounded

again. A fire had broken out next door to the Opera House. A high wind carried the flames to the Opera House itself and on to the brick-constructed building of Robert M. Wright and Company. The roof of the building caught, and the flames descended to gut the interior—then spread to adjoining buildings on the block. As soon as the ruins cooled, Dodge began rebuilding, determined to carry on.

But when a third fire broke out near the depot, destroying property and merchandise worth thousands of dollars, it seemed as if some avenging spirit was intent on reducing the town to ashes. In fact, the Reverend W. G. Elliot said as much from his pulpit the following Sunday: "God is venting His wrath on Dodge City for its manifold iniquities."

In contrast to the scourge of fire came the bitter cold of an unusually severe winter. On New Year's Day a raging blizzard swept into town, and that night buried the city under two feet of snow. Before Dodge could dig itself out, the storm attacked again, with more snow and a twenty-degree-below zero temperature. No mail or supplies came through on the Santa Fe; the civic-minded Ham Bell led an army of citizens with shovels to dig out the last train buried beneath twelve-foot drifts of snow. Cattle froze by thousands on the range, hogs died in their pens, sheep's carcasses lay scattered on the Plains.

Some verses quoted by J. Frank Dobie express the effects of that "unspeakable winter."

> I may not see a hundred
>   Before I see the Styx,
> But, coal or ember, I'll remember
>   Eighteen eighty-six.

> The stiff heaps in the coulee,
>   The dead eyes in the camp,
> And the wind about, blowing fortunes out
>   As a woman blows out a lamp.

These disasters did not mark the end of Dodge— it was made of sterner stuff. The city emerged like a phoenix from the ashes of catastrophe. Its golden era was waning, but much of its old-time fighting spirit lingered on. In an unusual gunfight between lawmen of the town, Mysterious Dave Mather settled a personal feud with Thomas Nixon by shooting him dead outside the Opera House. Charged with murder and released on bail, Mysterious Dave skipped town allegedly disguised in "petticoats and hooped skirt." The *Globe* further reported, "His whereabouts will probably become known when it comes time for his next killing."

But in general the old-time gunmen, gamblers, outlaws, and dance-hall girls were leaving Dodge for greener pastures, and once-raucous Front Street was being patrolled by "mumbling Ben Hodges carrying an old revolver locked fast with rust."

For the true gunslinging renegades, as well as action-seeking marshals, were moving on to cities not yet tamed. Here they acquired other identities, other reputations, good or bad, and ended their days by means that were fair or foul. Mysterious Dave Mather, for example, after fleeing Dodge, ended up as city marshal of New Kiowa, Kansas, where, as last reported, he was "making a good officer."

Wyatt Earp, after quitting Dodge, prospected for gold in Idaho and California, became a private detective for a while, refereed boxing matches (Tom Sharkey versus Bob Fitzsimmons in 1896), and after the turn of the century retired near Los Angeles to tend his modest ranch and write his memoirs. "The greatest consolation I have in growing old," he wrote, "is the hope that after I'm gone they'll grant me the peaceful obscurity I haven't been able to get in life." He died peacefully in his sleep in 1929, just short of his eighty-first birthday, and today near the Colorado River stands the town of Earp, named in the former marshal's honor. And, as one might expect, there is a Wyatt Earp Boulevard in today's Dodge City, connecting with the old Santa Fe Trail.

Bat Masterson, after being voted "the most popular man in Dodge City" in a July Fourth ceremony in 1885, and awarded a gold-headed cane for this distinction, moved on to Denver. Here he managed a burlesque show and married a song-

and-dance girl; then, like Wyatt Earp, became involved in professional boxing as second and referee. He was in Jake Kilrain's corner when the latter lost the heavyweight championship to John L. Sullivan in Mississippi. President Theodore Roosevelt, who had met Bat on a Western tour and knew of his reputation, offered him the job of United States Marshal for the State of Oklahoma (and later the same post for the Southern District of New York), but Masterson declined the honor. In words reflecting the sad passing of the Old West, Bat wrote the President:

> I am not the man for the job. Oklahoma is still woolly, and if I were marshal some youngster would want to try to put me out because of my reputation. I would be a bait for grown-up kids who had fed on dime novels. I would have to kill or be killed. No sense in that. I have taken my guns off, and I don't ever want to put them on again.

After the turn of the century Bat moved on to New York, where, though he had never got beyond the eighth grade, he became sports writer for the *Morning Telegraph* and died at his desk on October 25, 1921, at the age of sixty-eight. A newspaper columnist wrote a memorial:

> A plainsman bold has just passed on,
>   A man of the Last Great West;
> Fighter and hunter and great old scout,
>   They have laid him away to rest.

Billy Tilghman resigned as marshal of Dodge in 1885 to operate a stock farm near the city. The *Western Farmer* hailed him as "a perfect gentlemen, highly respected, who in the past brought law and order to Dodge City." But he became involved in several shooting sprees, in one of which he gunned down self-styled "bad man" Edward Prather. Whether or not Tilghman was at fault, he decided to leave the area. When Oklahoma was opened to settlers in 1889, he joined the land rush and was one of the first to stake a claim in the new territory. But for the generally mild-mannered Billy, who had rarely drawn a gun unless he had to, it was the end of the trail. He was shot dead by a drunken prohibition agent in 1924.

Ham Bell lived out his life in Dodge, serving a total of eighteen years as lawman in the city, perhaps the longest term on record, acting in one interval as mayor. Jim "Dog" Kelley also remained in Dodge, continuing to run the famed Dodge Opera House. Chalkley Beeson served for a while in the Kansas state legislature, hunting antelope on the side with his famous greyhounds. His wife and son later established the Beeson Museum, containing mementoes of the Old West, now a tourist attraction in Dodge City.

After leaving for Fort Worth, Texas, gambler Luke Short achieved dubious distinction by gunning down Long-haired Jim Courtright, former marshal of that

town. The judge ruled justifiable homicide; but it
was Luke's last killing. He turned scholar and
burned the midnight oil in reading Longfellow,
Byron, and Shakespeare—dying of dropsy with his
boots on in 1893. Doc Holliday's end had been
foreordained. With nothing to lose but his life, Doc
continued his reckless career of gambling, drinking,
and killing in Southwest frontier towns, until he
himself was brought down by tuberculosis in a
Colorado sanatorium in 1895.

Of the more notorious gunmen of Dodge City,
the end was equally predictable. Ben Thompson,
for example. After killing Jack Harris, operator of
a gambling hall in San Antonio, and accusing
another gambler named Joe Foster of cheating him
at cards, Ben made a curious mistake. With his
occasional weakness for generosity, he retracted his
charge against Foster and offered to shake hands.
In reply, Foster shot him five times in the head,
killing him instantly.

Clay Allison, the would-be assassin of Wyatt
Earp, died even more ingloriously. Posing, with
wife and child, as a respectable cattle raiser on the
Washita River in Oklahoma, Clay stole the heavily
loaded freight wagon of a friend. The wagon struck
a pothole, Clay was thrown from his seat, and a
wheel passed over him, breaking his neck. Jack
Allen's last killing, the shooting of Cockeyed Frank
Loving (murderer of Levi Richardson) in Colorado,

led to his conversion to the Christian faith. He became a traveling evangelist and preacher, exhorting his gunslinging followers to seek salvation.

Of the more than thirty million buffalo that had roamed the Plains of Southwest Kansas and had helped to build Dodge City in the first place, a single-sentence epitaph suffices. "You may hunt long and diligently in Kansas," wrote James Marshall in 1945, "without finding a single skull or robe"; while the two great buffalo hunters, Wild Bill Hickok and Buffalo Bill Cody, spent their later years touring the country in Ned Buntline's Wild West Show. By then, however, it was rumored that Wild Bill had become so blind that he could not hit a barn door with a rifle.

The Great Plains Indians who had shared the prairies with the buffalo, and were now confined to dwindling reservations, were given a moment of hope by their medicine man, Wovoka. By the eclipse of the moon in 1889 Wovoka had a vision: the white man would sink beneath the sod, and the Indian and buffalo would again be in possession of the Plains. To implement this vision he led his people in the ritual of the ghost dance; even the great chief Sitting Bull paid homage to this Indian messiah and his new religion.

All over the Plains the ghost dancers swayed from dawn to dusk, in passionate belief of their return. Until Indian agents and army officers became alarmed. The ghost dance and the Indian revival must be stopped! And so—Sitting Bull was shot outside his cabin, and the U. S. Cavalry pursued the ghost dancers as far as Wounded Knee Creek two hundred miles from the Kansas border, and massacred almost all of them: two thirds were women and children. The bright hope which Wovoka had rekindled in the hearts of the Great Plains Indians died with the martyrs at Wounded Knee.

By this time Dodge City was enjoying undistinguished peace and quiet as an agricultural and ranch community. In 1888 the editor of the *Western Farmer,* as if reporting on some ancient, long-dead civilization, wrote: "Years ago Dodge City was the most noted border ruffian town on the face of the earth. Today it has the reputation of a first-class moral, civil and religious city." True, Dodge was fast changing its image, due partly to its loyal, old-time citizens.

Bob Wright, the Merchant Prince of Dodge, bequeathed to the city the multi-acre Wright Park, with its zoo containing five Longhorn cattle and a pavilion named for George M. Hoover, who left his liquor and wheat fortune of one hundred thousand dollars to the city. Dr. Thomas L. McCarty and his son Claude established the first hospital in Dodge in 1903, using a converted three-story boardinghouse for the purpose. Dr. O. H. Simpson, the dental surgeon, left many of his sculptures to the town. One, the life-size statue of a Texan cowboy, a model of Sheriff Sughrue, still overlooks the quiet little city on the Plains.

How does one end the story of Dodge City? Perhaps one doesn't. For Dodge lives on—not only in popular imagination as an enduring symbol of the West, but in so many forms of dramatic entertainment, movies, fiction, radio, and television. Since Warner Brothers produced the film *Dodge City* in 1938, Dodge and its characters have afforded material for numerous motion pictures (*My Darling Clementine, Gunfight at the OK Corral, Hour of the Gun,* and more recently Frank Perry's *Doc*). On television, Gene Barry has portrayed Bat Masterson; and while there is no Matt Dillon listed in the annals of Dodge City, *Gunsmoke,* laid in Dodge and roughly based on the life of Wyatt Earp, has had a longer run than any other dramatic series in television history.

And of course Dodge City itself remains as something of a reigning queen among the quiet towns of Kansas; its streets paved with brick and lined with butternut trees, its pleasant houses embraced by New England-type lawns and shrubbery, and its seventeen thousand citizens going peacefully about their businesses. Boot Hill still stands, with its Hanging Tree, though those formerly interred there have been moved to other cemeteries. There is a wax museum portraying life-size figures of such Dodge City characters as Doc Holliday, Belle Starr, Bat Masterson, and Wyatt Earp. And there is also a replica of Front Street and a few of its old-time establishments, where mock gunfights are staged for the benefit of summer tourists. Somewhere is posted Zane Grey's apt quotation: "Along the two blocks known as Front Street was enacted more frontier history than anywhere else in the West."

But best of all quotations on Dodge City, in this writer's mind, is one which contains no claims to fame or boastful language. In 1878, when Dodge was at the height of its reputation as Queen City of the Great Southwest, the editor of the local *Times* observed: "Kansas has only one Dodge City. There is only room for one."

One might go further today and add that in the story of the West there is only one Dodge City. And to understand that story, there is need for only one.

Bibliography

Adams, Andy, *The Log of a Cowboy*. Boston, Houghton Mifflin, 1903.

Bradley, Glenn D., *The Story of the Santa Fe*. Boston, Gorham Press, 1920.

Breihan, Carl W., *Great Gunfighters of the West*. San Antonio, Naylor Co., 1962.

Brown, Dee, *Bury My Heart at Wounded Knee*. New York, Holt, Rinehart & Winston, 1970.

Brown, D., and Schmitt, M. F., *Trail Driving Days*. New York, Bonanza Books, 1952.

Connelley, William E., *Wild Bill and His Era*. New York, Press of the Pioneers, 1933.

Cook, John R., *The Border and the Buffalo*. Topeka, Crane & Co., 1907.

Cox, William A., *Luke Short and His Era*. New York, Doubleday, 1961.

Crumbine, Samuel J., *Frontier Doctor*. Philadelphia, Dorrance, 1948.

Cultural Heritage and Arts Center, *Dodge City, Queen of the Cowtowns*. Dodge City, 1970.

Dobie, J. Frank, *The Longhorns*. Boston, Little, Brown, 1941.

Dodge City *Times*. News reports and editorials in weekly issues subsequent to 1876.

Drago, Harry S., *Notorious Ladies of the Frontier.* New York, Dodd, Mead, 1969.

——, *Wild, Woolly and Wicked.* New York, Clarkson Potter, 1960.

Duffus, R. L., *The Santa Fe Trail.* New York, Longmans, Green, 1931.

Dykstra, Robert R., *The Cattle Towns.* New York, Knopf, 1968.

Fletcher, Sidney E., *The Cowboy and His Horse.* New York, Grosset & Dunlap, 1951.

Ford County *Globe,* Dodge City. News reports and editorials in issues subsequent to 1878.

Foy, Eddie, and Harlow, A. F., *Clowning Through Life.* New York, Dutton, 1928.

Gard, Wayne, *The Great Buffalo Hunt.* New York, Alfred Knopf, 1959.

Haines, Francis, *The Buffalo.* New York, Thomas Y. Crowell, 1970.

Hammond, Dorothy, *The Dodge City Story.* New York, Bobbs-Merrill, 1964.

Hertzler, Arthur E., *The Horse and Buggy Doctor.* New York, Harper, 1938.

Hough, Emerson, *The Passing of the Frontier.* New Haven, Yale University Press, 1918.

Jahns, Pat, *The Frontier World of Doc Holliday.* New York, Hastings House, 1957.

Karolevitz, R. F., *Doctors of the Old West.* Seattle, Superior Publishing Co., 1967.

Lake, Stuart N., *Wyatt Earp, Frontier Marshal.* Boston, Houghton Mifflin, 1931.

Lowther, Charles C., *Dodge City, Kansas.* Philadelphia, Dorrance, 1940.

Lomax, John A., *Cowboy Songs and Other Frontier Ballads.* New York, Macmillan, 1918.

Marshall, James, *Santa Fe: The Railroad That Built an Empire.* New York, Random House, 1945.

Masterson, William B. ("Bat"), *Famous Gunfighters of the Western Frontier.* Fort Davis, Frontier Book Co., 1968.

Miller, N. H., and Snell, J. W., *Great Gunfighters of the Kansas Cowtowns,* Lincoln, University of Nebraska Press, 1963.

Mora, Joe, *Trail Dust and Saddle Leather.* New York, Scribner's, 1946.

Nicholas, Alice, *Bleeding Kansas.* New York, Oxford University Press, 1954.

Raine, William MacLeod, *Famous Sheriffs and Western Outlaws.* New York, Doubleday, Doran, 1929.

Rath, Ida Ellen, *The Rath Trail.* Wichita, McCormick-Armstrong, 1961.

Rollins, Philip A., *The Cowboy.* New York, Scribner's, 1926.

Rosa, Joseph G., *They Called Him Wild Bill.* Norman, University of Oklahoma Press, 1964.

Schmidt, Heini, *Ashes of My Campfire.* Dodge City, Dodge City Journal, 1952.

Strate, David K., *Sentinel to the Cimarron*. Dodge City, Cultural Heritage and Arts Center, 1970.

Streeter, Floyd Benjamin, *Prairie Trails and Cow Towns*. Boston, Chapman & Grimes, 1936.

Swessinger, Earl A., *Texas Trail to Dodge City*. San Antonio, Naylor, 1950.

Thompson, George G., *Bat Masterson: The Dodge City Years*. Topeka, Kansas State Printers, 1943.

Tilghman, Zoe A., *Marshal of the Last Frontier*. Glendale, California, Arthur H. Clark, 1949.

Vestal, Stanley, *The Old Santa Fe Trail*. Boston, Houghton Mifflin, 1939.

———, *Queen of Cowtowns: Dodge City*. New York, Harper, 1952.

Watkins, Ethel E., *Annie, Child of the Prairies*. Colby, Kansas, Prairie Printers, 1968.

Webb, Walter Prescott, *The Great Plains*. Boston, Ginn & Co., 1931.

Wiggins, Owen D., *The History of Dodge City, Kansas*. Thesis submitted for degree of master of arts, Colorado State College of Education, Greeley, 1938.

Wright, Robert M., *Dodge City, the Cowboy Capital, and the Great Southwest*. Wichita, Eagle Press, 1913.

Index

Hunters, 8, 13, 164; bounty, 183; buffalo, 19ff., 30, 42, 46–47; trophies, 93. *See under* Buffalo
"Hurrah" the town, 46, 60

Indians, 3, 12, 54, 57, 79, 82ff., 155, 166, 168, 267–68; Apaches, 81; Arapahoes, 81; bases of civilization, 18; Cherokee, 46, 75; Cheyennes, 7, 8, 81, 87, 116, 222, chiefs, 90, 94, 95, 222; Chief Sitting Bull, 267–68; Comanches, 7, 18, 81, 82–83, 87, 165, 180; Coronado, 16; cowboys, 85ff., 95; hunting grounds, 84, 87; Kiowas, 81, 94, 201, chief, 87, 94; medicine men, 87, 91, 267–68; nostrums, 164–65, 171; Plains, 24, 32, 84, 87, 94, 180, 267, number, 81; ponies, 80, 81–84; raids, 7, 9, 93ff.; reservations, 81, 94–95, 267; subjection, 94–95; Territory, 3, 24, 84, 85, 88, 92, 168, 189. *See* Adobe Walls, battle

Jordan, Kirk, 13, 42–43

Kansas, 1–3, 5–6, 11, 92, 94, 113, 131, 206; governor, 235; laws, 259; motto, 15; name, 3
Kelley, Jim "Dog," 44, 72, 123–24, 126, 201–2, 231, 265; Earp, 216–18; mayor, 78, 96, 150, 152, 154, 194–95, 211–12, 214, 215, 226
Kenedy, James "Spike," 124–26
King Ranch, 124, 210
Klaine, Nicholas, 98, 232

Lake, Stuart, 50, 67, 143, 221
Law enforcement, 40–42, 63, 64–78, 126; officers, 67, 71, 102, 110, 132, 147–48, 151–52, 187, 190, 210ff., 219, 226, 240
Leslie, Frank, 131, 143
Lind, Jenny, 123
Louisiana, 9; Purchase, 4
Loving, Frank, 147–48, 222, 254, 266
Lowe, Rowdy Kate, 119, 251

McCarty, Dr. Thomas L., 126, 147, 167–68, 169–70, 173, 174, 177, 221, 268
Marshals, 13, 41–43, 46, 47, 65, 136, 150, 183, 226; guns, 102
Masterson, Ed, 26, 46, 65, 69, 71, 72, 75–77; death, 77, 78, 211, 212, 218
Masterson, Jim, 65, 75, 189, 212, 228–30
Masterson, William "Bat," 13, 26, 46, 65, 68, 70ff., 76, 77–78, 83–84, 86, 89, 93, 97, 152, 159, 185, 212, 220, 226, 229–30, 236–38, 240, 253, 259, 263, 270; death, 264; friends, 157, 160; guns, 102, 103, 108–9, 111, 123; religion, 248, 250, 253; roles, 131, 132, 134, 138; sheriff, 110, 125–26, 141, 182, 189, 190, 217, 218; TV, 269
Mather, "Mysterious Dave," 29, 46, 65, 75, 247, 262, 263
Mexicans, 140, 182, 207
Mining camps, 14, 156, 176
Morrow, Dave "Prairie Dog," 28–29, 75, 189, 252
Movies, 103, 130–31, 193, 269
Music, 193, 204–5, 207, 208, 244, 245

New Orleans, 121, 123, 159
New York City, 9, 20, 27, 38, 258, 264

West, 127; entertainers, 232–33, 238, 239, 258, 262; guns, 117–18; legendary, 116–17; pioneer mother, 129; religion, 244, 247–49

Wright, Rev. O. W., 122, 124, 152, 246–47, 249–51, 254

Wright, Robert "Bob," 14, 17, 23, 28–29, 36, 40, 41, 42, 58, 79, 82, 92, 96, 194, 212, 216, 225, 231, 246, 268